SEXUALLY TRANSMITTED DISEASES

SEXUALLY TRANSMITTED DISEASES

by
Alan E. Nourse, M.D.

FRANKLIN WATTS
NEW YORK LONDON TORONTO SYDNEY

Illustrations by Vantage Art
Photographs copyright ©: World Health Organization: pp. 21
(A. Zuckerman), 23 (Institut Pasteur, Paris), 43, 86; UPI/Bettman
Newsphotos: pp. 33, 45, 54, 103; Photo Researchers, Inc.: pp. 61 (SIU),
81 (NIBSC/SPL); National Institute of Allergy and Infectious Diseases/
NIH: pp. 69, 73, 95, 97; F & M Projects (from STD Bulletin 1990,
Vol. 9 No. 5, p.6): p. 109; Bettye Lane: p. 113.

Library of Congress Cataloging-in-Publication Data

Nourse, Alan Edward.
Sexually transmitted diseases / by Alan E. Nourse.
p.   cm.
Includes bibliographical references and index.
Summary: Explains sexually transmitted diseases, treatments for them,
and means of prevention.
ISBN 0-531-11065-6
1. Sexually transmitted diseases. [1. Sexually transmitted
diseases.] I. Title.
RC200.N68   1992
616.95'1—20
91-21707 CIP AC

CONTENTS

*This book is not intended as a substitute for the
medical advice of physicians or public health
counselors. The reader should consult a physician in
matters relating to sexually transmitted diseases or
other aspects of his or her health, and particularly in
respect to any symptoms that may require
diagnosis or medical attention.*

Want to get frisky? Don't want to pay the price?
Just fill it up with whiskey and pack it down with ice.
   Oh, roll her over,
   Give her Coca-Cola.
   A dish of ice cream,
   Lemon soda,
But it takes soap and water, baby, for to keep it
clean.*
                    —*Dave Van Ronk*, "No Dirty Names"

---

* Traditional scat song from the 1930s, additional lyrics and arrangement by Dave Van Ronk, BMI.

1
STDs: WHAT ARE THEY?

This book is about *sexually transmitted diseases*—the kind of infections that are passed on from one person to another during sex. These diseases are often called "STDs" for short. They are especially important infections for young people to know about, because they can cause you an awful lot of very unpleasant trouble. Most of them can be treated and cured once they are diagnosed—but some of them can't. And many of them can cause long-lasting complications if they *aren't* discovered and treated. Some can even be fatal.

Fortunately, *all* of them can be prevented—if you know how to do it. The purpose of this book is to tell you all about these infections, and how you can protect yourself against them.

INFECTIONS AND INFECTIONS

The world is full of different kinds of infections. When you cut your finger, it may become sore and swollen

9

because the cut has been seeded, or *infected,* by germs from the surface of your skin. Such minor infections happen all the time. Everybody occasionally catches a head cold or flu, too. These are infections caused by germs that are breathed out into the air by infected persons or are transmitted through hand-to-mouth contact. And most people know about diarrhea (loose bowel movements) caused by germs growing in spoiled food or contaminated water. Infections of this sort are an ordinary fact of life. Everybody gets them now and then, and nobody is particularly shy talking about them.

Sexually transmitted diseases are different. These diseases are also infections, spread by a variety of different germs. But nobody ordinarily talks about them very much. The reason is that the germs that cause STDs are all usually passed from one person to another by sexual contact, and most of them affect the sex organs directly.

Not everybody gets these infections. In most cases, you only get an STD by having sex—and then only if you're unwise or unlucky enough to have sex with somebody who already has a sexually transmitted infection to pass on to you. Some people imagine that they will only catch an STD if they have sex frequently with lots of different partners, but that's just not true. Such people *do* run a higher than average risk of becoming infected— but a person can just as easily catch an STD by having sex just once with just one partner, if that one partner happens to be infected.

You may never even have heard of some of these sexually transmitted infections. But it's very important that you know about them. Although a few of them are mostly just nuisances, others are really dangerous. Many of them can cause very unpleasant symptoms, as well as lasting damage to your body. Any one of them can turn your life into a real mess.

TROUBLE WITH STDS

Sexually transmitted diseases can affect people's lives in many different ways, almost all of them unpleasant. For example, consider the problems STDs caused for four young people very much like yourselves. (Their names have been changed, but the stories are true.)

Just four months ago Gail T., age fourteen, started going steady with the most popular boy in her class. She thought it was great that a really cool guy like Tom seemed to like her so much. They started having sex almost immediately. Everything went fine for a couple of months—but then Gail started feeling sick. She began having severe stomach pains and cramps. Almost every afternoon she ran a temperature of 101° F. Having sex with Tom began to be painful, and she seemed to have a lot of discharge all of a sudden. Naturally, she couldn't tell anybody about something like this, so she just toughed it out for a couple of months. Finally, her mother realized how sick she was and insisted on taking her to a doctor.

Gail T. had an STD known as **gonorrhea**. Like many girls, she hadn't noticed any symptoms at first. But soon the infection had spread from her vagina and cervix, where it had started, up into her tubes. (We'll talk more about the sex organs affected by STDs in the next chapter.) This caused a kind of internal swelling and soreness that her doctor called **pelvic inflammatory disease** or **PID**. Laboratory tests revealed the cause: a germ that is known to cause gonorrhea. The doctor ordered some medicine for Gail, and in a few days the pain, cramps, and fever were gone. But she still had to be checked from time to time to be sure the infection was completely cured. And to her embarrassment, Tom also had to be examined and treated for the same infection. As a result, Tom didn't come around anymore—which may have been just as well for Gail.

Actually, Gail was very lucky that she got so sick she had to get help early. Sometimes a gonorrhea infection in a girl will just sit quietly and smolder for months and months without causing many symptoms at all. But during that time, it can damage a girl's tubes so badly that she may never be able to get pregnant later. Untreated gonorrhea is one of the major causes of *infertility* (the inability to have a baby) in young women.

Greg H., at the age of sixteen, got in trouble with an STD during his summer vacation at the beach. He and his buddies met some girls cruising on the boardwalk one night and ended up having a great all-night beach party, complete with sex and all. Greg never saw the girl again, but ten days later his hips began aching, and the next day he found a little cluster of very painful, itchy blisters on his penis.

Greg's father suspected the worst and took him to a doctor. A lab test showed that Greg had been infected with **genital herpes**. The doctor ordered a salve that helped quiet down the infection, but a month later it came right back again. Greg then had to start taking some very expensive medicine called **acyclovir** to help prevent the infection from recurring. Of course, scientists know that a genital herpes infection doesn't kill otherwise healthy young people, or cause any permanent serious harm to the body. But it doesn't go away either, and it can't be cured. For Greg, this infection will be a painful, embarrassing nuisance that may come back to bother him again and again for years to come. If nothing else, it will certainly interfere with his sex life in the future. The really sad thing is that Greg could easily have protected himself from this infection, if he'd known about it in time and had taken the right steps to live defensively.

12

Josh W., age twenty-two, has a much more serious problem. Just recently home from the navy, he and his girlfriend Marcie were planning to get married. But when they had the premarital blood tests their doctor recommended, Josh's test came back positive for **syphilis**. Marcie wasn't exactly pleased with this news, and Josh was horrified. True enough, he'd had sex with quite a number of different girls while he was in the service. But he'd never had any symptoms that he could remember. (The early signs of syphilis, one of the most dangerous of all STDs, are often easily overlooked.) The truth is that Josh was very lucky his doctor insisted he have that premarital blood test. The results haven't helped his wedding plans very much, but at least he has now been treated and cured of the infection. Without treatment, syphilis could have caused enormous and irreparable damage to Josh's body and brain over the years. It might very well finally have killed him—and in the meantime, Marcie could have been infected, too, without even knowing it.

At age sixteen, Sue K. is suddenly terrified and doesn't know what to do. She's known all along that the biker she's been riding with for the last year has been shooting up drugs. But now she's heard that one of his closest buddies has developed AIDS. She knows that her guy and his buddy had frequently used the same needle for shooting up together. Sue knows the virus called HIV that causes AIDS is often passed from one person to another with dirty needles—and now she's heard it can also be passed on through sex.

Imagine the questions in Sue's mind! Could her boyfriend be infected? Could *she* be infected because of having had sex with him? He hasn't been sick and refuses to have a test for HIV infection—it couldn't happen to *him*, he says. Should *she* have a test? She's read that not many girls get HIV disease this way, but that some do. What if she's one of them? She can't talk to her parents about something like this. Who *can* she talk to? Suddenly Sue is faced with some very serious and frightening questions—and she doesn't have any idea where to turn for help.

KNOWING ABOUT STDS

These four young people have quite different problems. But they all share two things in common. All of them have been having sex, and all four of them have been exposed to sexually transmitted diseases. Unlike other infections, these diseases have a way of thoroughly messing up people's lives—sometimes permanently.

Some of you may be thinking, "Why pick on *young* people about this? Don't older people get these diseases, too, and spread them around?" Of course they do. But the fact is that young people—high-school and college students—today are at greater risk from STDs than anyone else. The United States Public Health Service reports that diseases such as gonorrhea, syphilis, and genital herpes have been spreading very rapidly all over the country in the last ten or fifteen years—and they are *spreading far more rapidly among teenagers than in any other age group.**

Why is this? For one thing, today more and more teenagers are having sex earlier and earlier than was once the case. That means that more and more of them are exposed to these diseases, and the risk of catching them becomes greater and greater. For another thing, not many young people know very much about these diseases, or how to protect themselves from STDs, or

---

* See J. W. Zylke, "Interest Heightens in Defining, Preventing AIDS in High-Risk Adolescent Population," Medical News and Perspectives, *Journal of the American Medical Association,* October 27, 1989—Vol. 262, No. 16, p. 2197.

how to prevent them from spreading. Finally, teenagers tend to be far more reluctant than older people to do anything about it when they *do* suspect they may have such an infection. The overall result is that these infections are spreading like wildfire in this particular age group—an age group that doesn't have very much knowledge or experience to deal with them.

It doesn't have to be this way. But changing things depends on *you*. Your first and best defense against STDs is to *know that they exist*—and to know something about them. In this book we'll talk about what these infections are, what causes them, what symptoms to watch for, and what to do if you think you might be infected. Then we'll see what active steps you can take to protect yourselves from these infections. A good place to start is with the tiny troublemakers that cause STDs in the first place, and the sex organs that generally become infected.

2
THE TINY
TROUBLEMAKERS

Where do infections of any kind come from?

More than three hundred years ago, a Dutch lens-grinder named Anton van Leeuwenhoek made a crude microscope by putting a small, high-powered glass lens into a tube. His "microscope" was really nothing more than a powerful magnifying glass, but in the year 1677, by peering at a drop of pond water through this tube, Leeuwenhoek made a remarkable discovery. He found that the water droplet was full of tiny living creatures too small to be seen with the naked eye. Because some of these creatures seemed to move around on their own, he called them "animalcules" or "little animals."

Today we know that some of these animalcules are tiny plants. Others are tiny animals. Still others seem to be somewhere in between. Scientists now call them all *microbes* or *microorganisms,* terms which simply mean "very small living things." Most people just call them "germs."

During the 1800s and early 1900s a number of brilliant scientists began learning more and more about

16

these germs. The most famous of these "microbe hunters" was the French chemist Louis Pasteur, who lived from 1822 to 1895. Among many other discoveries, Pasteur proved that some of Leeuwenhoek's animalcules could cause human infections. Another famous scientist, the German bacteriologist Robert Koch, showed beyond a doubt that certain specific germs always cause certain infections. For example, in 1882 Koch discovered the germ that causes the dreaded lung disease tuberculosis, and proved that tuberculosis is transmitted by one person spreading the germ to another person.

Germs exist everywhere in the world. They live in our rivers, ponds, and oceans. They float in the air we breathe. They live on our skins, on the objects we touch, in our food, sometimes even inside our bodies.

Most of these microorganisms are harmless to us. Many of them have good, useful work to do, like the germs that decay rotting leaves and turn them into rich soil. But some, if they find their way into our bodies, can grow and multiply there and cause **infections**. These particular germs are called *pathogens,* or "disease-makers." There are several different kinds, and each kind causes trouble in a different way.

THE BACTERIA

Microorganisms in one large group are called *bacteria.* These are tiny, one-celled plantlike organisms. They cannot be seen with the naked eye, but they're quite large, as microorganisms go. Most can be seen under a microscope, especially when they have been colored, or stained, with a red or deep purple dye to make them show up better.

Some bacteria are round or oval in shape. Doctors call these bacteria *cocci. Streptococci* or "strep" germs grow in long chains and cause severe throat infections. *Staphylococci* or "staph" germs grow in clusters like

17

grapes and cause pimples and other skin infections. Our skin is literally covered with these germs. A number of different kinds of *diplococci* or "double cocci" grow in pairs. One kind cause a dangerous infection of the spine and brain called *meningitis*. Others, called *pneumococci,* cause a very serious kind of lung infection known as *pneumonia*. And still another kind, the *gonococci,* live best on the warm, moist surfaces of the male and female sex organs. They are passed from one person to another during sex and cause the harmful sexually transmitted disease called gonorrhea.

Other bacteria can also cause STDs. Some, called *bacilli,* are shaped like rods. One group, known as *Hemophilus ducreyi* or Ducrey's bacilli (named after the dermatologist who first identified them), cause an uncommon STD called **chancroid infection**. Much more common is a very dangerous STD known as syphilis. This is caused by spiral-shaped bacilli called *spirochetes*. They look like little corkscrews under the microscope. They are very hard to see because they won't soak up any of the usual dyes to make them stand out. Doctors or lab technicians have to use microscopes equipped with special backlighting, or "dark-field," light sources to see them at all. This can make the syphilis germs very difficult to detect directly.

What do bacteria *do* that's so bad when they invade the body? First they begin damaging cells and tiny blood vessels in the area they enter. Some manufacture dangerous *toxins,* or poisons, as they multiply. To fight them off, the body sends in armies of special *white blood cells* to try to destroy them. The area where this battle is fought becomes swollen and sore, and the body temperature may rise. A *fever* usually means that an infection has started somewhere in the body.

Sometimes the white blood cells win this battle. The bacteria are killed, and the body begins to heal the damage. This is what happens when a sore throat often gets better after a few days even when you haven't taken anything for it. But in many cases the bacteria aren't killed. The infection spreads. The germs may get into the bloodstream and cause *septicemia* ("blood poisoning") and spread to distant organs. There they continue to grow and multiply. This may sometimes lead to harmful infections in the lungs, the kidneys, the bones or joints, the brain, the liver, or other organs.

Before 1936 there wasn't much doctors could do to fight infections. Many people died of such infectious diseases as diphtheria, pneumonia, whooping cough, or bad strep infections—all caused by bacteria. Then a chemical called *sulfanilamide* was discovered. It prevented certain dangerous bacteria from growing. By the early 1940s drugs such as *penicillin* and *streptomycin* had been found and put into use. These drugs actually killed bacteria and cured many infections. They were called *antibiotics*, and today we have dozens of antibiotics to cure dangerous infections.

How important are antibiotics to our health? Their discovery was probably the most important step forward in all medical history. Medical historians believe that in prehistoric times, as many as 60 percent of all people died before the age of twenty-five or thirty because of infectious diseases. Today, thanks to antibiotics, a death from infection is an uncommon tragedy.

Fortunately, some antibiotics will kill the bacteria that cause STDs such as gonorrhea or syphilis. But these infections must be discovered and treated early, before too much damage has been done.

THE VIRUSES

Viruses are a completely different kind of germ. They are the tiniest of all microorganisms, so very small that they can't be seen at all under an ordinary microscope. Scientists can only visualize them photographically with an electron microscope.

Viruses are also the simplest, most primitive of all

living things. Some scientists wonder if they are really "living" at all. A virus is nothing more than a tiny bit of hereditary material called DNA or RNA, wrapped up in a protective envelope made of protein. Viruses can't multiply on their own, the way bacteria or other micro-organisms do. All a virus can do is make its way inside the living cells of some other creature, and then force those cells to make more viruses.

All the viruses we know are *parasites*. That means they force other organisms to keep them alive and don't do anything good in return. When they invade or *infect* other living cells, they not only force those cells to pro-duce more viruses, they usually kill the cells in the pro-cess. Then the newly made viruses go on to invade and kill other cells. The more viruses that are made, the more cells are killed. So when a disease-causing virus invades a human being, it can often cause a bad infec-tion. A flu virus, for instance, can destroy cells in the lung and cause a kind of pneumonia, sometimes severe enough to kill a person. A hepatitis virus can destroy cells in the liver and cause death from liver failure.

Fortunately, the human body can successfully fight off many virus infections before they become deadly. The body's natural *immune system* (a complicated army of protective cells and protein molecules known as *an-tibodies*) can often search out and destroy viruses. In many cases, the body's immune system remains alert after the virus is beaten off by making guard cells that carry the antibody molecules' pattern, so the virus can't come back and start another infection later. But other viruses are able to hide from the body's immune system by making protein coats that match normal body proteins—a kind of molecule camouflage—and never go away once they've gotten into the body.

Viruses cause many kinds of infections in people. Ordinary head colds, flu, measles, mumps, and chicken pox are all virus infections. And viruses can cause sex-

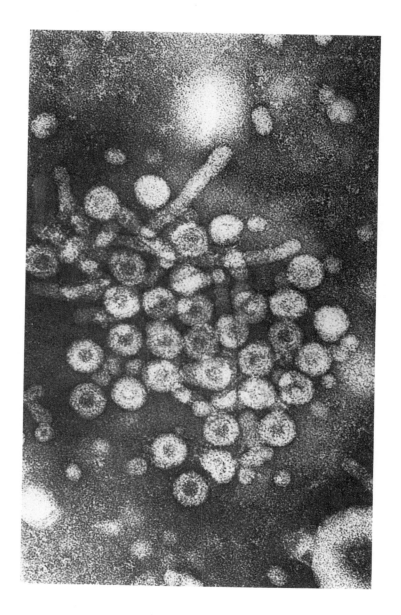

The hepatitis B virus as seen through an electron microscope

ually transmitted diseases, too. One STD caused by a virus is genital herpes. Another is known as **HIV disease** (**AIDS**), and still another as **hepatitis B**.

So far there are no drugs people can take that will kill viruses the way antibiotics can kill bacteria. The best we have are a few drugs that slow down the production of new viruses inside the invaded cells. This means that diseases like genital herpes or HIV infection are not curable. Sometime in the future, genital herpes or HIV infection may be prevented by vaccination shots, as measles and mumps are today. But so far no vaccine has been perfected to prevent either genital herpes or HIV infection.

OTHER TROUBLEMAKERS

There are a few other kinds of germs that can also cause STDs. **Protozoans**, for example, are tiny one-celled animal-like organisms. Malaria and African sleeping sickness are examples of very dangerous infections caused by protozoans. One protozoan named **trichomonas** can cause an unpleasant, annoying infection in the vagina. It can also infect the boy's penis. It is sometimes passed back and forth between two people who have sex frequently. This can make the infection very hard to get rid of.

Various **yeasts**, a kind of fungus, can also cause vaginal infections and be passed on to a sex partner. So can another germ, known as **chlamydia**. This is now believed to be the most common and fast-spreading STD in the United States today. Fortunately, all these STDs can be treated and cured with the proper medicines, once they have been detected.

THE TARGET ORGANS

In the case of most STDs, the sex organs themselves are the first targets of infection. Before we talk about the

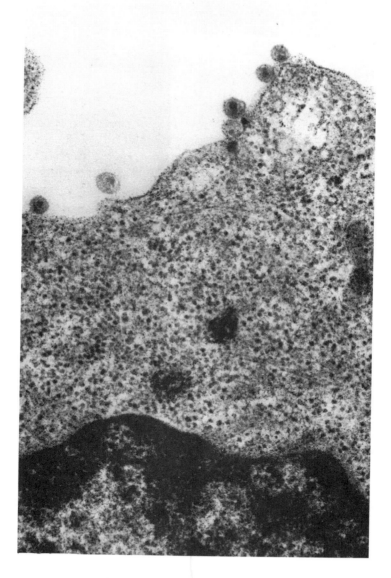

*The HIV virus as seen through
an electron microscope*

individual STDs, we need to review those target organs most likely to be hit by sexually transmitted infections.

Most of the boy's sex organs are located outside the body. The **penis** is a tube-shaped organ between the legs. When a male is excited about sex, his penis temporarily enlarges and becomes stiff with an **erection**. Behind the penis is a pouch of skin called the **scrotum** holding two oval sex glands, the **testicles**. They produce the sperm cells. Hollow tubes then carry the sperm up into the **pelvis** (the lowest part of the abdomen) for storage. During sex the sperm empty into the boy's urine tube, called the **urethra**. This tube carries the sperm down the whole length of the penis, to the outside. In a boy, most STD germs are likely to infect the penis first, or find their way up into the urethra and start the infection there.

A girl's sex organs are all inside her body except for the external entry to the vagina, which is called the **vulva**. The **vagina** is a stretchable internal tube or canal a few inches long connecting the vulva with the lower end of the **uterus** or womb. The uterus is shaped like a small pear, with a narrow lower end, called the **cervix**, and an upper part, the **body**. It has thick walls of muscle with a hollow space inside. A very narrow canal passes up through the cervix from the vagina into the space inside the uterus. This means that male sperm cells—and STD germs—can make their way up there from the vagina. At the top of the uterus the internal space connects with narrow tubes on either side, called **fallopian tubes** or **oviducts**. These tubes extend up to contact small glands called **ovaries** on either side. An egg cell must pass down one of the fallopian tubes, from an ovary toward the uterus, in order for a young woman to get pregnant. So it's important that those tubes don't get blocked or obstructed in any way.

When a girl is first infected by an STD germ, the infection may start on the external folds or **labia** of the vulva, or in the girl's urinary canal or **urethra**. But some

THE MALE
REPRODUCTIVE SYSTEM

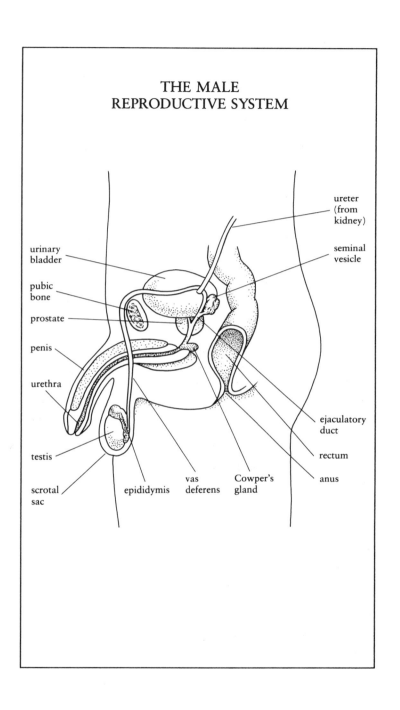

ureter
(from
kidney)

seminal
vesicle

urinary
bladder

pubic
bone

prostate

penis

urethra

ejaculatory
duct

rectum

anus

testis

scrotal
sac

epididymis

vas
deferens

Cowper's
gland

THE FEMALE
REPRODUCTIVE SYSTEM

uterus

fallopian tube

ovary

cervix

bladder

pubic bone

clitoris

rectum

anus

labia majora

labia minora

vulva

urethra

vagina

infections first affect the vagina or cervix, where they are harder to detect. Later, STD germs may work up through the uterus to cause an internal infection and blockage in the fallopian tubes, or around the ovaries. This can be a very common, painful, and harmful complication of an STD in a girl.

Of course, the germs that cause STDs don't necessarily attack the sex organs themselves exclusively. The genital herpes virus can cause sores to develop on the buttocks or thighs or anyplace else where infective sex contact occurs. The gonococci can attack the rectum or the throat as the initial place of infection. In fact, these gonorrhea infection sites are especially common among male homosexuals (male/male sex partners), as well as among heterosexuals (male/female sex partners) who engage in oral or anal sex practices. The syphilis spirochete can spread through the body, after initial infection, and grow destructively in virtually any organ. The primary targets of the HIV (Human Immunodeficiency Virus, or "AIDS virus") are special immune system white cells known as macrophages and T4 cells, and the hepatitis B virus mainly attacks liver cells. But in all of these cases, sexual contact remains the major way, or one of the major ways, that the germs are spread from person to person.

PINNING DOWN
THE VILLAIN

When a doctor suspects that a person may possibly have an STD (we'll talk about the signs and symptoms of these infections later), the first task is to be sure the problem really *is* an STD, and then to determine *which one*—usually by trying to identify the particular germ involved—in order to decide which treatment will work best. There are several different kinds of laboratory tests that can help pin down the villain.

1. When an STD is caused by bacteria, it is often possible to actually see the germ under the microscope and identify it that way. A bit of mucus from the infected area is spread on a glass slide. The slide is dipped in a staining solution, and then examined microscopically. The germ that causes gonorrhea, for example, is often easily spotted with this simple test. (The germ causing syphilis may be seen without staining under a specially lighted "dark-field" microscope.)

2. In some cases the bacteria can best be found by spreading a bit of infected material on a *culture plate* coated with a nutrient material to help the bacteria grow. The plate is then placed in an incubator at body temperature for a day or two. When tiny colonies of growing bacteria appear on the plate, they can be spread on a slide, stained, and examined microscopically. This kind of culturing technique not only identifies the bacteria present, but has an added advantage as well. The bacteria growing on the culture plates can be exposed to a variety of different antibiotic drugs to determine directly which drugs will do the best job of killing those particular bacteria, and which ones will no longer work because the bacteria have become *resistant* to them. (We'll say more about the problem of antibiotic-resistant bacteria in chapter 3.)

3. Blood tests of various kinds can sometimes detect the presence of an STD even when the germ can't be found directly. For example, a blood test called a **serological test for syphilis** or **STS** can reveal an active syphilis infection within a few weeks even when the person has noticed no warning symptoms whatever.

4. Modern **antibody assays** are now used to detect other hidden STDs, especially those caused by viruses. Unfortunately, most viruses causing STDs are extremely difficult to grow in cultures, and can only be seen under an electron microscope when they do grow. This kind of

28

procedure is *possible,* but it's very time consuming and expensive, and only a few laboratories are equipped to do it. So actually growing the viruses for identification in each individual case isn't usually practical.

Fortunately, there's another, much simpler, way for virus invaders to be detected. When viruses attack cells in the human body, the body's natural protective immune system begins manufacturing special protein molecules called *antibodies* to oppose and fight down the viruses. For each specific kind of virus which has invaded, a very specific, identifiable group of antibodies soon appear in the bloodstream. They don't show up instantly, but sooner or later the bloodstream is full of them. Once the body has made them, special tests called *assays* can be used to detect them. It doesn't matter that these tests don't detect the virus itself, directly. The fact that the antibodies are there in the blood stream tells us that *that* virus has already invaded that body sometime before.

Such tests are extremely important and useful, for example, when a very dangerous virus such as the Human Immunodeficiency Virus or HIV—the so-called "AIDS virus"—is involved. A positive HIV antibody test tells the doctor that yes, indeed, that person has been infected with HIV disease, whether he or she has any symptoms of AIDS yet or not. Knowing very early that that person has been infected with HIV, and may sooner or later develop symptoms of AIDS, can well be lifesaving. It may then be possible to use medicines to slow the growth of the virus in the body, and thus delay or even prevent the development of this deadly disease.

5. Finally, in very special cases, tests using advances in molecular biology can be used to pin down the presence of an STD.

Whatever the STD may be, it is important to detect the infection as early as possible. And since the person who has caught a sexually transmitted disease is likely

29

to be the first person who knows when signs or symptoms appear, it's important that everybody know some facts about these individual infections. In the following chapters we will see how the major STDs behave, what telltale symptoms can occur, and what can be done about them.

3
GONORRHEA

Two very different sexually transmitted diseases have been causing people trouble for many hundreds—perhaps even thousands—of years. They are gonorrhea and syphilis. Until the 1940s these two infections were considered especially dangerous public health problems: they were very widespread, and there were really no good, fast, reliable ways to treat or cure either of these diseases.

Then antibiotic drugs were discovered that could cure both diseases quickly and completely. For a while doctors thought that gonorrhea and syphilis would soon be wiped off the face of the earth. But no such thing happened. In fact, both infections today are rampant, and are attacking teenagers and young people more than any other age group. Since gonorrhea occurs far more frequently than syphilis—it's one of the most wide-spread of all STDs—and is particularly a plague among modern teenagers, we'll talk about it first.

31

DOUBLE TROUBLE

Everyone has heard of gonorrhea. Sometimes it's called "clap" "a strain," "a dose," or "GC." As you might guess from so many nicknames, lots of people have had lots of trouble with this infection. Over 733,000 new cases were reported in the United States in 1989, the latest year for which complete figures are available.* But this may be only a small part of the real problem. According to U.S. Public Health Service estimates, there were probably an additional 3.6 million new cases that same year that *weren't reported at all.* Unfortunately, more than two thirds of these new cases are occurring in teenagers and young people.

In a man, the gonorrhea bacteria usually first infect the urethra or urine tube. In a woman, it can also infect the urethra, but more often silently attacks the cervix first, and then later spreads to the body of the uterus and the Fallopian tubes. And in people who have oral sex or anal sex contacts, gonorrhea of the throat or rectum is common.

The infection is caused by small oval-shaped bacteria called *gonococci,* which grow together in pairs like twin coffee beans. When smeared on a glass slide, stained, and examined under a microscope, they appear bright scarlet. Bacteriologists tell us that gonococci are surprisingly frail organisms, as bacteria go. They can live only a short time outside the body, or on a dry surface. This means that nobody is likely to catch gonorrhea from a toilet seat, in spite of any stories you may hear. The germs are very hard to grow outside the body at all, even on special culture plates and under special laboratory conditions of warmth and humidity.

---

* Summary of Notifiable Diseases, United States 1989. U.S. Public Health Service, *Morbidity and Mortality Weekly Report,* Centers for Disease Control, Atlanta, Ga. 38, no. 54 (October 5, 1990).

A campaign launched by the state of Minnesota
to fight venereal disease used the slang name
for gonorrhea to get the message across.

But they grow very rapidly on the warm, moist surfaces of the sex organs, and are easily spread from person to person during sexual contact.

SIGNS AND SYMPTOMS
OF GONORRHEA

When a person has sex with someone who is infected, the gonococci can invade the sex organs of either sex. The germs then begin infecting the warm, moist cells lining these organs. Uncomfortable symptoms begin from a few days to one week after contact. A boy will usually notice pain when he passes his urine, and a thick, yellowish discharge from his penis. A girl may also have pain during urination, plus a yellow discharge from the vagina. This discharge usually increases in amount from day to day.

With this infection, there are no sores that you can see on the surface of the sex organs. This is one way to tell gonorrhea from genital herpes, where visible sores usually appear. With gonorrhea, the infection is internal. But simple lab tests will often show that the infection is there.

For example, a drop of the discharge from the penis or vagina is put on a glass slide and stained with dyes, using a method invented in 1884 by the famous Danish bacteriologist Hans Christian Gram, and now commonly known as a Gram stain. First the specimen is stained with a purple-colored dye. Then it is counterstained with a bright red dye. Gram discovered that certain groups of bacteria always retained the purple dye, and showed up purple-black when examined under the microscope. These bacteria are called *Gram-positive*. The strep and staph germs, and the pneumococci, are all Gram-positive. Other groups of bacteria, including those causing gonorrhea, always stain bright red, and are called *Gram-negative*. This difference provides a very reliable way of distinguishing between bacteria that might otherwise look very much alike under the microscope.

When gonococci are present in a specimen of discharge from an infected person, they show up clearly under the microscope as bright red, coffee-bean-shaped twin cocci mixed in with many pus cells (white blood cells that have been killed fighting the infection). Some of the germs are seen outside these dead cells, but some are also seen *inside* the cells, proving that the white cells had been trying to fight the infection by engulfing the invading germs.

This exam can easily confirm a diagnosis of gonorrhea, often right in a doctor's office, especially in the case of a boy. But in a girl's case, the germs may not be found just by examining a specimen of the discharge, so the doctor will also make cultures in order to grow and identify the bacteria if they are there.

Although the first symptoms of this infection are messy and uncomfortable, they aren't terribly painful. They may be even harder for a girl to notice than a boy. Sometimes people just pretend they aren't there. That's too bad, because this early stage of infection is the best time to treat and cure gonorrhea, before it has a chance to do serious damage. This is also the time when gonorrhea is *extremely contagious.* Any sex contact at this stage of infection is almost certain to spread the disease to the sex partner. If gonorrhea is discovered and treated at this early stage, it can be cured quickly (see "Treating and Curing Gonorrhea," below). But if the infection isn't discovered, or is ignored, serious problems can arise.

COMPLICATIONS OF GONORRHEA

One bad thing that can happen is that the germs, after growing and multiplying in the sex organs for a while, can get into the bloodstream and travel to the joints. There they can lodge and grow, causing a painful and damaging joint infection called *septic arthritis*. The knees are most frequently attacked, but the elbows or other joints can also be infected. Treatment can stop the infection at this point, too. But long-term damage to the joints may occur if treatment is delayed.

In a girl, untreated gonorrhea can cause another kind of long-term trouble. After a few days or weeks, the early infection may seem to quiet down, even without treatment. But it isn't gone. During this time, the germs can work their way up into the Fallopian tubes and start an infection there. This can cause fever and severe pain in the lower abdomen. As the girl's body tries to fight the infection, the tubes become swollen and filled with pus. Then scarring and blocking of the tubes can occur. Doctors call this pelvic inflammatory disease or PID. (As we will see, other bacteria can also cause PID, but many of the worst cases are due to gonorrhea.) Sooner or later the body may fight off this infection, or it may be cured by antibiotic treatment. But the scarring and blocking of the tubes will often remain to prevent the young woman's egg cells from traveling down the tube for contact with sperm cells. In many cases this can make her permanently *infertile* (unable to have babies).

In other cases, an egg cell may well be fertilized with a sperm cell, but then get stuck in a blocked segment of the tube and thus not get down to the uterus where the pregnancy belongs. In such cases, the fertilized egg cell may develop into a pregnancy right there in the tube. This is a very dangerous situation known as a *tubal pregnancy* or *ectopic pregnancy* (*ectopic* simply means "in the wrong place"). Tubal pregnancies can easily lead to sudden, life-threatening internal hemorrhage (heavy bleeding) and require emergency surgery.

Gonorrhea can also attack the babies of infected mothers. If a young woman has gonorrhea when her

36

baby is born, the germs can get into the baby's eyes and quickly cause blindness. Doctors or nurses now put drops of silver nitrate or antibiotics into every baby's eyes as soon as it is born, just in case the mother might have gonorrhea and not know it. These drops kill any bacteria present. They have saved the sight of thousands of babies over the years.

TREATING AND CURING GONORRHEA

Seeing how harmful gonorrhea can be, it's obviously important to treat it and cure it as soon as possible. Before antibiotics came along, treatment often involved thoroughly uncomfortable and often ineffective procedures such as squirting silver compounds up the urethra or into the vagina. There were also dozens of "home remedies" used, such as vinegar or whiskey douches, or ice packs—all completely useless—and you may well hear about some such remedies from your friends even today. Ignore them. None of them work. Fortunately, gonorrhea *can* be cured quickly and effectively with antibiotic drugs—but not always as easily as when antibiotics were first discovered forty or fifty years ago.

When penicillin was first discovered and used in the early 1940s, doctors found that a single large shot would cure gonorrhea almost overnight in more than 99 percent of the cases. The germ seemed to be very *sensitive* and was easily killed by this drug. But over the years, many gonococci became *resistant* to penicillin. This meant that certain of the germs that *weren't* killed by penicillin proceeded to multiply into families, or *strains,* of gonococci that could protect themselves from attack by that drug.

Doctors soon learned that when one of those strains of gonococci infected a person, penicillin didn't work very well against them—and sometimes not at all. Those people had to be treated with *tetracycline,* a different

37

kind of antibiotic. But after a while, strains of gonococci started appearing that were resistant to tetracycline as well. Today many cases of gonorrhea are resistant to both of those drugs, so doctors must often use still other antibiotics for several days or even longer to cure gonorrhea. And then the person must be checked from time to time after treatment to be sure the infection is completely gone.

When antibiotics are prescribed, it's extremely important for you to take them *exactly* as the doctor directs, and to take them *all,* until they are gone, not just until symptoms ease up. Many people stop taking the antibiotic after a couple of days, as soon as symptoms seem better, but then have the infection right back again a week later. And this, of course, contributes to the development of antibiotic-resistant germs, too, since it is the germs that can fight off the antibiotic the best that survive and multiply and cause the reinfection.

There's one other problem in dealing with this disease: although the body tries hard to fight down this infection, it doesn't develop any lasting immunity against the germs, so a person can be reinfected again and again with later exposures. With each new infection you have to start all over again with treatment. Two people who frequently have sex together can just reinfect each other time and again unless both are treated and cured at the same time to break this reinfection cycle.

Treating and curing both partners at the same time is also essential to prevent the spread of the infection to others. This means that an infected person has to be certain that his or her sex partner goes in for examination or treatment too. If necessary, at least the partner must be identified to the doctor or to Public Health authorities so that contact can be made. Of course, this can be an extremely embarrassing thing to have to do. I know perfectly well how difficult it is for young people to do what must seem to them like ratting on a friend—it may be the most difficult thing you've ever had to do. But however much you might dislike this idea, I hope you'll do it anyway, because it is so very important. It may be the only way your friend can be spared the dangerous complications of a thoroughly nasty infection. It may prevent *you* from being reinfected later. It's the *only* way that the continuing spread of gonorrhea in your school or community can be slowed down. And let's face it: it's really one of the adult responsibilities you take on when you decide to have sex. Fortunately, Public Health officials do their best to keep this "case-finding" procedure as confidential as possible—so it doesn't have to become public knowledge.

Of course it would be good news if a vaccine could be found to protect people from gonorrhea. But so far no such vaccine has been developed. The best protection anyone has today is *prevention*. We'll talk about how to prevent gonorrhea and other STDs in chapter 9.

WHAT TO DO?

What should you do if you suspect you may have a gonorrhea infection? The first step is to see some medical professional just as soon as possible, since timing is so important in stopping the infection. Any doctor in practice anywhere is well acquainted with this infection, and knows how to diagnose it and treat it. If you already have a family doctor who knows you—a doctor whom you like and trust—that could be the best place to start. According to medical ethics, any doctor should respect your confidence—that is, he or she should help you deal with the problem without telling your parents or anyone else about it without your permission. Unfortunately, that doesn't always work out in practice. Even when the doctor respects your confidence, others in his office are likely to see your medical record. Those people are also bound by the same rules of confidentiality that the doctor is, but common sense tells us that the more people who know about a secret, the more chance somebody else is going to hear about it.

This matter of confidentiality is extremely important here. Teenagers often feel that they're not regarded as full-fledged, adult citizens. They're often extremely reluctant to discuss very private, personal matters with adults. How many of your friends have *you* heard saying, "I just couldn't talk to anybody about something like that," or "My dad would kill me if he knew I was having sex"? When it comes to something like a sexually transmitted infection, even knowing how dangerous it can be, young people often don't know *who* to trust, so they don't trust anybody, and don't do anything about the problem until it gets so bad that they're forced to. This is obviously one major reason that STDs are spreading so rapidly in teen populations today—because these young people aren't doing anything about these infections when they first turn up.

Where STDs are concerned, there are no all-purpose answers to this. But there are some steps you *can* take to protect your privacy and still get prompt, effective help. If you are going to see your family doctor, or some other doctor, talk with him or her about this question of privacy *first,* before you describe your problem. Don't just sit there with your mouth closed. Make certain that the doctor clearly understands your desire for privacy, and assures you that he'll cooperate, or if he won't, *why* he won't. If you're not completely satisfied and comfortable with that doctor's response, walk out and find another doctor.

Fortunately, there's another alternative that you can consider, too. Sexually transmitted diseases are widely recognized as a public health menace. It's important to *everybody* that an infected person be treated and, if possible, cured. Every community in the country, large or small, has access to a Public Health Department. Every Public Health Department either has, or has access to, a publicly supported STD clinic where people can go to be diagnosed and treated for STDs under conditions of privacy. Any Public Health nurse or other Public Health employee can direct you to the nearest such clinic. You can find Public Health telephone numbers listed in your local phone book, or in the phone book of the nearest medium-sized community or county seat. What is more, Public Health Department STD clinics will provide diagnostic and treatment services at no cost to you if you don't have the means to pay.

It may be that you, personally, would feel more secure going this "anonymous" route than going to a private doctor. It doesn't really matter, as long as the job gets done without delay. Even a Public Health clinic will need to know who you are, and may well ask you to identify the person you caught the infection from, if possible, as a matter of protecting that person and the rest of the world.

There's no way around it: getting help diagnosing and treating gonorrhea or any other STD is likely to be a big, fat bother. As we pointed out first thing in this book, these diseases have a way of making a mess of people's lives, in more ways than one. That's why it's so important that you know about them and how to protect yourself from them. But your continuing good health takes first place over anything else. If you think you might have a gonorrhea infection, or any other STD, don't put off getting help. Just grit your teeth, face the problem, and get something done about it fast.

4
SYPHILIS: THE "GREAT IMITATOR"

The precise time when many serious infectious diseases first appeared on earth is lost in the clouds of history. Leprosy, for example, was well known in biblical times, along with a number of other diseases that were mistaken for leprosy but probably weren't—nobody knows exactly when true leprosy first appeared. Medical historians suspect that the great plague that struck in ancient Greece during the Peloponnesian Wars between Athens and Sparta around 430 B.C. was really a virulent form of red measles. And both smallpox and bubonic plague were known long before A.D. 1000, and may have been present in early Roman times.

With syphilis, it was a different story. We know that this infection—still one of the most dangerous of the sexually transmitted diseases—first appeared in Europe quite dramatically in the late 1400s or early 1500s as a dreadful killer. No one knows exactly where or why it started, but it spread throughout Spain, France, Italy, and Central Europe in a vast epidemic within a matter of a few decades. This was a time of incessant wars in Europe, and the disease was carried far and wide by armies of soldiers and their infected camp followers.

42

A seventeenth-century engraving that says
"The Spaniard with Naples Disease."
This patient with syphilis is undergoing a
treatment that involved powdering the skin.

Nobody cared to claim responsibility for it—Italian soldiers called it "the French Disease," French soldiers called it "the Spanish Disease," and so forth. More generally, it was called "The Great Pox" to distinguish it from another terrible killer, smallpox.

Then, as now, syphilis was spread by sexual contact. It got its medical name from the story of a mythological Greek shepherd named Syphilus, who insulted Apollo; for this, the story goes, the angry god afflicted him with a loathsome disease. And indeed, at the time it first appeared, syphilis was considered so disgusting that doctors wouldn't even write its name down, using the Greek letter sigma (Σ) as a symbol for it. Even today some medical students use Σ in their lecture notes as shorthand for syphilis.

Why did such a disease appear so suddenly, and where did it come from? Nobody knows for sure. Some historians think it had long been present as a mild, relatively unnoticed disease, and then suddenly became virulent, possibly because the germ that caused it had *mutated,* or changed, in some way. Others speculate that the disease might actually have originated in the New World, among Native Americans in the Caribbean and Mexico, and had been brought home by Spanish explorers. They point out that Columbus's historic voyages occurred just a short time before the disease appeared in Europe. Probably, at this late date, we will never know for sure.

What *is* certain is that in those days syphilis was a swift and terrible killer. Early in the infection, victims developed raging fevers and open, weeping, infectious sores on the skin. Many people died in the first days of their infection. For those who survived this first stage, the destructive ravages of the syphilis germ later moved rapidly throughout the body, with deadly effect. The overall death rate from the disease at that time was very high.

*A South American Inca clay figure
shows the ravages of syphilis.*

Syphilis today is not as virulent as it was in those terrible times. Nobody knows for sure why that should be. Perhaps the germ that caused it mutated or changed again, or perhaps, over the centuries, the human immune system has simply learned to cope with the infection better. Early stages of the infection today are mild, but the late, destructive stages, which can occur years after the initial infection, are still extremely dangerous—and deadly.

Syphilis is still very much alive today. In 1989 there were over 107,500 cases of syphilis reported in the United States—44,500 "new cases" discovered in the primary or secondary stage of infection, plus another 63,000 "late-stage" cases discovered in the same year, as well as 859 cases in newborn babies.* And of all the sexually transmitted diseases, syphilis is one of the most dangerous—far more so than gonorrhea.

Why is it so dangerous? For one reason, because *Treponema pallidum*, the germ that causes syphilis, can do so much damage to the body if the infection isn't discovered and treated early. Unfortunately, it often isn't. It's easy to miss the earliest signs of the infection, or mistake them for something else. But unless detected early, the germ of syphilis soon "goes underground" to distant parts of the body. There the infection can spread silently for years. It can slowly attack the brain, the spinal cord, the blood vessels, or other organs, causing terrible destruction or even death.

THE STAGES OF SYPHILIS

Treponema pallidum is a tiny corkscrew-shaped bacterium. It's actually a very delicate germ that will only live a short time on a dry surface outside the body, but it

---

* *Morbidity and Mortality Weekly Report,* Centers for Disease Control, Atlanta, Ga. 38, no. 54 (October 5, 1990).

thrives in the warm, moist tissues of the sex organs, and can make its way into the body without any break in the skin. It is passed from one person to another during sex.

The first or **primary** *stage of infection.* Once contact is made, this germ can burrow through the moist surface layers of the penis or vulva and start growing in cells just beneath the skin. The first sign of infection usually appears some ten to twenty-one days or more after infectious contact. It is a small, painless ulcerlike sore called a *chancre.* This usually forms somewhere on the sex organs. It may be on the penis, or the vulva, or even somewhere inside the vagina. It is often so unimpressive that the person may not even notice it, and because it isn't painful you can easily miss it completely. Even if you do notice it, you might mistake it for genital herpes, except that it doesn't hurt the way genital herpes does (see chapter 6 for more about genital herpes).

Syphilis is very contagious, or easily spread, at this stage. As long as the chancre is there, it is teeming with spirochetes, so the infection can be passed on to anybody else the infected person has sex with. But this first or *primary* stage of syphilis doesn't last very long. If you don't do anything about it, the chancre will heal and go away all by itself in a matter of four to six weeks. Unfortunately, the infection *doesn't* go away—the spirochetes are still there, growing and spreading.

The second or **secondary** *stage.* While the chancre is healing, the spirochetes have been multiplying rapidly and spreading to all parts of the body. For a period of time the infection remains *latent*—present but silent and hidden. Then, sometime between one and six months later, a reddish-brown skin rash may appear all over the body. Sometimes shallow ulcers will also appear on the lips, in the mouth, or inside the cheeks. This rash marks a second, more widespread stage of infection called *secondary syphilis.*

If everybody with syphilis developed this kind of full-blown secondary syphilis rash, the disease would be

47

easy to detect at this stage. Unfortunately, everybody doesn't. In some cases the rash doesn't appear at all, or may be so slight as to escape notice. But whether the secondary syphilis rash is noticeable or not, the infected person at this stage is again extremely contagious, and can pass the infection along to anyone by sexual contact.

Soon, however, this rash also disappears, all by itself, as if it had never happened. But by now a change has taken place in the body. Starting about ten days after first infection, the infected person's immune system begins to react to the invasion, and antibodies—special immune proteins—begin appearing in the person's bloodstream. These antibodies are hand-tailored by the immune system to help fight and destroy the spirochetes (which, of course, are "foreign invaders" in every sense of the word).

The appearance of these antibodies at this point is important for two reasons. First, soon after they appear, the antibodies can be detected by a simple blood test known as a *serological test for syphilis* or STS. If you are found to have a positive STS, this is a tip-off that you have—or have had—an active syphilis infection which is probably still going on in your body. The test is so simple and widely available and inexpensive that most doctors order it as part of the routine laboratory work done whenever a person has a complete physical examination. Many previously undetected cases of syphilis are picked up in this way. This is fortunate, because the person can then be treated immediately, before the disease goes any further. The STS is the basis for the familiar *premarital blood test* that used to be required before a marriage license could be issued. This requirement has now been discontinued in most states, but the test is still universally recommended by doctors for people about to be married. It's just plain commonsense self-protection.

Even more important, the antibodies are at least partly effective in fighting the spread of the spirochetes in the body. Experts now believe that in about 30 percent of all new infections—that is, in three out of ten cases—the body's immune system with its antibody armies actually *win the battle* then and there. The spirochetes are either wiped out all at once, or else are slowly destroyed following the secondary stage of the infection. Those lucky people recover without any treatment and remain free of the disease, unless they are reinfected by another sexual exposure later.

The remaining 70 percent, however, may not be so lucky. In their bodies, the infection may be slowed down, but it is not completely wiped out. And about one third of these people go on to develop dangerous and often fatal late-stage syphilis months or even years later, unless the infection is somehow detected and stopped in the meantime.

*The third or **tertiary** stage of syphilis.* In these people, the skin rash of secondary syphilis gradually goes away in a month or so, but the spirochetes don't. They just "go underground" in the body. There is another long, latent stage of the disease in which nothing seems to happen; there is no visible evidence of trouble. The only sign of infection during this latent phase is that the serological test for syphilis remains positive. This "silent" or latent stage can go on for months or even years. But then, sooner or later, signs of late-stage or *tertiary* syphilis begin to appear.

Late-stage syphilis can reveal itself in a variety of different forms, many of which may seem to mimic or imitate other diseases. In fact, late-stage syphilis is sometimes called "The Great Imitator." For example, a man might suddenly discover that he can't walk properly in the dark without seeing his feet. He can no longer feel the floor under him, because the spirochetes have permanently destroyed nerve cells in his spinal cord. Doc-

49

THE STAGES OF UNTREATED SYPHILIS

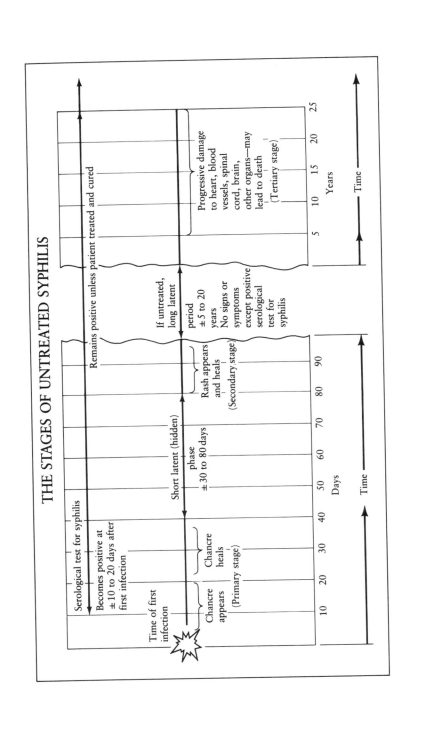

Serological test for syphilis

Becomes positive at ±10 to 20 days after first infection

Remains positive unless patient treated and cured

Time of first infection

Chancre appears (Primary stage)

Chancre heals (Primary stage)

Short latent (hidden) phase ±30 to 80 days

Rash appears and heals (Secondary stage)

If untreated, long latent period ±5 to 20 years No signs or symptoms except positive serological test for syphilis

Progressive damage to heart, blood vessels, spinal cord, brain, other organs—may lead to death (Tertiary stage)

Days

10 20 30 40 50 60 70 80 90

Time

Years

5 10 15 20 25

Time

tors call this condition *tabes dorsalis,* and people who develop it are called *tabetic.* In other cases, spirochetes may destroy nerve cells in the brain and lead to a slowly deteriorating mental state known as *general paresis.* These people, who are called *paretic,* gradually lose their memories, can't think straight, can't speak clearly, or can't tell where they are or what day or year it is. These symptoms are typical manifestations of late-stage *neurosyphilis.*

In still other victims, the heart and great blood vessels are the target of the spirochetes. The germs can attack the wall of the aorta (the great artery in the chest), weakening it until it bulges out into a balloon-shaped *aneurysm* that may presently burst and cause sudden death. Or the heart muscle itself may be softened and weakened by a festering inflammation teeming with spirochetes. In fact, no organ system is safe from attack. The liver, the bones, the kidneys, or any other organ may be ruined in this late stage of the infection.

Obviously, syphilis is not an infection to be trifled with. Fortunately, today, it can be treated and cured, once it has been detected—and the earlier this happens, the better.

HOW SYPHILIS IS DETECTED

A person should suspect syphilis anytime a sore appears on the sex organs (the primary stage of the infection) or anytime a completely unexplained skin rash appears (the secondary stage of the infection). In either case, the spirochete itself is present in great numbers in the chancre, or in the area of the rash, and can often be identified directly, under the microscope, thus pinpointing the diagnosis. Because the germ won't absorb ordinary stains, this examination requires a microscope with very special backlighting and a lab technician who is experienced in identifying the spirochete. This so-called *dark-field exam* is usually done at an STD clinic or Public Health Service laboratory.

Often, however, the germ just can't be found. At the primary stage, the doctor then has to go on the history of the contact and the appearance of the chancre, unless the serological test for syphilis has already become positive by then. At the secondary stage, the skin rash has a very characteristic look about it, unlike almost any other skin rash. In addition, an STS blood test is almost certain to be positive at this stage. In either case, the doctor may decide to treat the patient then and there, on suspicion, even without an absolutely certain diagnosis.

Latent and late-stage syphilis are often first detected when a routine STS blood test proves positive. Such patients must be actively treated even though there are no symptoms at all. Other cases are first detected when neurological or other symptoms begin, or sometimes even by sheer accident: a doctor orders a routine chest X ray, for example, and the film reveals a large balloon-shaped bulge in the aorta. Treatment of late-stage syphilis stops the process of destruction that is going on, but it can't repair the damage already done. That's why it is imperative to detect and treat this disease at the earliest stage possible.

CURING SYPHILIS

Before the early 1940s syphilis was a very difficult infection to treat. Historically, the best treatment available was prolonged, painful treatment with compounds of heavy metals such as mercury, bismuth, or arsenic, all of which were fairly nasty poisons with very unpleasant side effects. In the late 1800s and early 1900s the great German bacteriologist Paul Ehrlich became interested in finding a drug to kill *trypanosomes,* the germs that caused African sleeping sickness. He was looking for a "magic bullet"—a medicine that would destroy the germ without damaging the body at the same time. In 1910 he came up with an arsenic compound that he named salvarsan 606, so-called because it was the six hundred and sixth such compound that he had tested! Salvarsan (now known as *arsphenamine*) didn't work against trypanosomes, but it turned out to be very good at killing the spirochetes of syphilis.

Ehrlich's discovery of salvarsan proved to be one of the great landmarks of medical history, for it marked the beginning of modern *chemotherapy* (a word coined by Ehrlich himself). For the first time a chemical remedy for a dangerous disease had been sought out and discovered by scientific techniques.

Salvarsan could cure syphilis. It worked slowly, and was still very toxic—but it was the best there was at the time. Then finally, in the early 1940s, came the careful study of *penicillin,* an antibiotic that Sir Alexander Fleming had first discovered quite accidentally in 1928, and the *real* "magic bullet" against syphilis was found.

Fortunately, most syphilis germs are killed very quickly by penicillin. Just one large dose of this drug is usually all that is needed to cure the infection. And fortunately, the syphilis germ is one disease-causing organism that has *not* yet developed widespread resistance to penicillin. A few cases have been reported in which penicillin didn't work, but not very many—the treatment is still very reliable. But some people are allergic to penicillin. For them, other antibiotics must be used, and will work just as well. In either case, this is such a dangerous infection that blood tests should be repeated later, after treatment, to be certain the infection is gone.

Interestingly enough, when penicillin is given to treat a primary or secondary syphilis infection, some patients have a very abrupt, dramatic reaction: sudden, profuse sweating, chills, and prostration that lasts for several hours. This so-called *Herxheimer reaction* is

*Sir Alexander Fleming, the Scottish
bacteriologist, was the first to
discover the drug penicillin.*

harmless enough, but it is startling, to say the least. Doctors believe the reaction is caused by large amounts of foreign protein suddenly released all at once into the bloodstream from dead syphilis germs that have been wiped out by the antibiotic.

CONGENITAL SYPHILIS

Sometimes even innocent babies can fall victim to syphilis. If a young woman with syphilis becomes pregnant, the spirochetes in her blood can infect her baby before it's even born. The child then has *congenital syphilis* at birth.

There has been a marked increase in cases of congenital syphilis in recent years. Of course, it is treated the moment it is detected, but serious harm may already have been done to the baby's body. For this reason, a blood test for syphilis is usually run the first time a woman sees a doctor about her pregnancy. If she has unsuspected syphilis, she will be treated immediately, to protect both her and her baby. And, indeed, the best way to reduce the number of cases of congenital syphilis is to be sure that *all* pregnant women have adequate prenatal care starting as soon as they know they are pregnant. Repeated STS blood tests and speedy treatment during the pregnancy will then ensure that the baby won't be infected.

THE CONTINUING EPIDEMIC

If syphilis can be cured so swiftly and completely with inexpensive medicines like penicillin, then why do we still have an ongoing epidemic of this nasty disease? Why hasn't syphilis been wiped out completely by now, the way, say, smallpox has?

First, of course, syphilis has to be detected before it can be treated, and that's part of the problem. As we saw earlier, it isn't always easy to detect the early stages of syphilis, unless you're very watchful. This is especially true in women, where the primary chancre may be hidden in the labia or the vaginal lining.

Second, you *don't develop immunity to syphilis.* Lots of people think that if you've had a sexually transmitted disease and have been cured, you can't get it again. That's not true of *any* STD, and certainly not true of syphilis. *Reinfection is very common,* and just as dangerous and easily transmitted to others as the first infection.

Third, syphilis is most prevalent among people who have lots of different sex partners, and who don't know much, or *do* much, to protect themselves against infection. This isn't just confined to prostitutes and their customers, although that is one major source of infection. It also includes a great many teenagers and college students who are busy enjoying their newfound sexual freedoms and aren't paying much attention to the risks. And as we have already seen, the majority of new cases turning up today are in these groups of people.

One final factor is that syphilis seems to vary in its infectiveness and virulence at different times. We've seen that it was exceptionally deadly when it first appeared in Europe in the 1500s, and then seemed to quiet down some. In modern times, there was a widespread epidemic of more virulent syphilis in the United States during the 1920s and 1930s, and then the disease again seemed to quiet down. We may or may not now be on another rising wave of virulence—but who wants to contract this infection and find out?

Perhaps the biggest factor of all in the syphilis epidemic today is that sexually active young people are simply not putting safe-sex practices into action. Syphilis can be prevented by the very people who are in the greatest danger of getting it. We'll talk in detail about self-protective measures *you* can take to keep from getting syphilis—and other STDs—in chapter 9.

56

5
CHLAMYDIA INFECTIONS AND OTHER STDs

Gonorrhea and syphilis are very widespread sexually transmitted diseases, and practically everybody knows they exist. But there are other STDs you may never have heard of at all. Some of these are fairly uncommon, at least in this country (although their incidence is rising among teenagers). But at least one—a very sneaky and dangerous infection, and a major cause of infertility in women—may be more widespread today than all the other STDs put together. This one is known as *chlamydia infection*.

CHLAMYDIA

Until about fifteen years ago, even doctors didn't know very much about this sexually transmitted infection. But today, some medical experts say it is the most widespread of all STDs. Certainly it is one of the hardest to detect; a lot of people who are infected just don't know it. And it's one of the most worrisome of STDs because of the way it can interfere with a young woman's ability to have children later.

Chlamydia is a sexually transmitted infection caused by a tiny germ known as *Chlamydia trachomatis*, about halfway in size between small bacteria and large viruses. These organisms are so small they can't be seen under an ordinary microscope. This means other lab tests are needed to detect chlamydia infections. This very same germ also causes *trachoma*, an eye infection that causes blindness. A very similar germ causes *psittacosis* or "parrot fever," a kind of pneumonia people get from infected birds. And a close cousin to this germ causes another quite different STD known by the jawbreaking name of *lymphogranuloma venereum*.

As in all other STDs, the chlamydia germ can infect both boys and girls. In a boy, the symptoms are a lot like gonorrhea, but they don't turn up so soon after exposure. Somewhere between seven and twenty-eight days after contact, the boy starts having pain and burning with urination, and has a thin, whitish discharge from his penis. If a drop of this discharge is studied under the microscope and no gonorrhea germs are found, the doctor will suspect a chlamydia infection. Some years ago this infection was known as "nongonorrheal urethral infection" and wasn't thought to be a sexually transmitted disease at all. Today we know better.

In about two cases out of three in a young man, these symptoms gradually disappear within three or four weeks, even without diagnosis and treatment, but he still harbors the germ and can infect or reinfect his sexual partners. In about one third of cases, however, complications may force him to seek medical help. These complications, especially common in young, sexually active men, may include *epididymitis*—a painful infection of the sperm-carrying tubes in the scrotum—or *urethral stricture*, in which scarring of the infected urine tube partially blocks the outflow of urine.

The situation is different in young women. They may have no symptoms at all except a slight vaginal discharge—no pain, burning, or other discomfort. This is because in girls the chlamydia germ most often infects the cervix—the lower end of the uterus or womb. If she happens to have a *pelvic exam* (an internal examination of her sex organs) at this time, the doctor may see a white discharge on her cervix. Lab exams of this discharge would then reveal the infection. But without any symptoms to bother her, she might have no reason to see a doctor. This means that many early chlamydia infections in young women are just plain overlooked.

Unfortunately, the infection doesn't go away. Untreated, it spreads up through the uterus into the tubes. There it causes a pelvic inflammatory disease, or PID, much the same as the PID caused by gonorrhea. The tubes become infected, swollen, and inflamed. At that time the girl may begin having lower abdominal pain or cramping—sometimes mistaken for menstrual cramps— and may develop a mild fever. If she should become pregnant at this time, she is likely to have a dangerous *ectopic pregnancy.* (This is a pregnancy that starts growing in a tube instead of in the uterus where it belongs.)

Later, as her body tries to heal the tubal infection, scarring can occur, blocking the tubes completely and causing permanent *infertility,* or the inability to become pregnant. Some experts now believe that undiscovered chlamydia infections are largely responsible for the recent great increase in the number of young women in their early twenties and thirties who can't seem to get pregnant, no matter how hard they try. Fortunately, these symptoms of PID may lead the girl to visit a doctor or an STD clinic in time for diagnosis and treatment before irreparable damage has been done.

DETECTING AND TREATING CHLAMYDIA INFECTIONS

If doctors can't see the chlamydia germs under the microscope, how can they tell the infection is there? One way is to *culture* or grow the germs into colonies in the laboratory and then identify the colonies with various chemical tests. Cultures, of course, take time to grow, so this method of detection is slow. Recently, special antibody tests and fluorescent staining techniques have been developed so that labs now can detect the chlamydia germs directly from smears taken from infected persons.

As for treatment, the chlamydia germs are enough like bacteria that a number of different antibiotics can cure the infection once it is detected. Tetracycline, doxycycline, and erythromycin are commonly used. But treatment takes time—at least seven days of medication—and many people relapse and must be retreated again later, so follow-up is important. Like most other STDs, a person *doesn't develop immunity* to a chlamydia infection by having it once. This means that reinfection is very common, especially when both the male and female partners are infected. Only by treating both partners at the same time can such "back-and-forth" reinfection be prevented.

When a woman with an active chlamydia infection has a baby, there is a serious risk that the baby's eyes will be infected by the germ at the time of birth. For this reason, hospitals routinely treat newborn babies' eyes with antibiotics immediately after birth. (This of course protects the babies from gonorrhea infection, too.)

One of the very sneaky things about chlamydia is the fact that the germ can hang around in the body for a long time without necessarily being noticed. With STDs like gonorrhea or syphilis, the ones most likely to be infected are people who are *promiscuous*—that is, people who are having sex with lots of different partners. Those people know perfectly well why they've been "singled out" for those infections. But chlamydia often appears in people who are *monogamous*—that is, people who have really had only one or two sex partners in their lives. Such couples aren't *expecting* to have any STDs. They are often appalled to learn that they *do* have a chlamydia infection, and don't understand how they

60

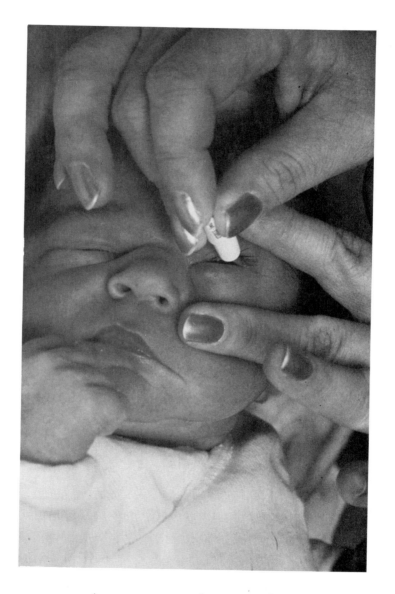

A nurse puts erythromycin drops in a newborn's eyes to prevent infection from chlamydia.

could have become infected. The truth is that a single exposure of either partner, years before, could be the source of infection now, even if the exposure may have been forgotten altogether.

TRICHOMONAS

This sexually transmitted infection is really more of a nuisance than a danger. An infection with **trichomonas** doesn't do any serious harm, except that it's very uncomfortable for the girl. Like chlamydia, it is quite widespread. And because of the genital itching and burning it causes, it is sometimes confused with another STD, genital herpes.

The germ is a protozoan called *Trichomonas vaginalis,* which lives and multiplies especially well in the vagina. It doesn't cause any blisters or sores. It just produces a thin, milky vaginal discharge that causes severe itching and burning. Since the germ is quite large, it can easily be seen under the microscope in a doctor's office or clinic. Once diagnosed, there are some simple medicines that will cure a trichomonas infection in most cases. The drug of choice is an antiprotozoan chemical known as *metronidazole* (trade name Flagyl) taken by mouth in pill form.

The treatment works, but it may not be permanent. For a long time "trich" was thought to be exclusively a female infection. Today we know the male can have the infection, too, without having any symptoms. This means that sex partners can easily pass the infection back and forth. It doesn't do much good to treat and cure the girl alone, because she is likely to be reinfected the next time she has sex with her partner. To get rid of this nuisance, both partners need to be treated at the same time.

In one sense, a trichomonas infection in a young woman is more than just a nuisance, however. She and her doctor today depend upon periodic Pap tests to detect early signs of cancer of the cervix, one of the most common female cancers. The presence of a trichomonas infection can interfere with the detection of abnormal cells in these Pap tests—it can hide the presence of the telltale abnormal cells in some cases, or make normal cells look abnormal in others. For this reason, if a woman is found to have a trichomonas infection, a Pap test should be done *after* it has been treated and cured, in order not to miss early signs of a much more serious disorder. (See p. 94 for more detail about Pap tests.)

THREE BAD ACTORS

Three other very unpleasant STDs need to be mentioned here. Fortunately, they haven't appeared very often in this country until quite recently. But they are on the upswing, especially among sexually active teenagers, Each one has its own special symptoms and requires a doctor's attention when symptoms appear.

One, known as **chancroid infection**, is caused by a large Gram-negative (red-staining) bacillus known as *Hemophilus ducreyi* or Ducrey's bacillus. This germ produces large, painful sores on or near the sex organs of either males or females. The lymph nodes in the groin also become swollen and tender. Sometimes these sores are confused with genital herpes, but a doctor can easily tell the difference. Chancroid infection can be cured quickly and completely with antibiotics. But if left untreated sores can extend into surrounding areas and cause a great deal of damage and scarring.

Another bad actor, **granuloma inguinale**, is caused by another bacillus. It is a slow-moving infection that spreads deep under the skin around the sex organs, causing painless beefy-red lumps and swellings. If left untreated, the infection spreads and spreads, causing widespread destruction of tissue in the area and severe

63

scarring. This infection is most often found in tropical and subtropical climates, so it isn't often seen in the United States. Like chancroid infection, it can be cured by antibiotics, but takes longer to heal.

The third of these infections, known as **lymphogranuloma venereum**, or **LVG** for short, is also most common in tropical countries, but recently has been appearing more and more in the United States as well. It is caused by a close cousin to the germ that causes the chlamydia infections we discussed earlier. But it results in quite a different kind of infection. The germ invades lymph glands in the groin or around the sex organs and causes very painful pus-filled swellings called **buboes**. This infection can be treated and cured with the same antibiotics used for chlamydia infections.

Of these three bad actors, chancroid infection is becoming epidemic among sexually active teens in the United States, but the others can also turn up once in a while. The main message about them is this: *Anything* that causes painful sores, lumps, or swellings on or around the sex organs requires a doctor's attention. These infections will cause permanent damage and trouble only if you ignore the symptoms and don't get medical help.

6
GENITAL HERPES

By now, everybody has heard about this STD. Fifteen years ago, hardly anybody knew very much about it, not even doctors. Not that it's a *new* infection—it's been around a long time. But until a dozen years ago, it just wasn't very widespread. Many people didn't recognize it, and nobody talked about it.

All that has changed now. Today genital herpes has exploded into a full-fledged epidemic. It is spreading very fast, especially among teens and young adults. It is now possible to control symptoms and recurrences of this infection with medicines, but there is no cure—once you're infected, you're infected for life. So it's important for young people everywhere to know some basic facts about this unpleasant infection:

1. It is a sexually transmitted disease—that is, it is spread from person to person by sexual contact.

2. It is one of the most widespread of all STDs today, particularly among teenagers and young people.

3. Though it doesn't usually kill anybody, or do dangerous things to the body, it *does* cause very unpleasant, painful, and recurring symptoms.

4. Once a person has genital herpes, it can't be cured and it doesn't go away. It just hides in the body forever. This means it can cause new attacks of symptoms, again and again, without advance warning, even after treatment.

THE GENITAL HERPES VIRUS

Genital herpes is caused by a virus called *herpes simplex virus #2* or just HSV2. This is a germ so very tiny that it can only be seen with a special electron microscope. It is a close cousin to another virus called *herpes simplex virus #1* or HSV1.

These two viruses invade the body through tiny scratches in the skin. Then they set up infections in the skin cells. HSV1 usually causes infections called *cold sores* on the lips or around the nose. But HSV2 invades the skin cells on or near the sex organs. Once inside those skin cells, HSV2 viruses force the skin cells to make more viruses very rapidly. When the infected areas break down into sores, the newly made viruses can then be passed on to other people during sex.

FIRST SYMPTOMS OF GENITAL HERPES

The first symptoms of genital herpes usually appear from two to seven days after having sex with someone who is actively infected. Very often the person will first notice a dull aching in the hips, low back, or legs for a day or so, and may run a slight fever. Then one or more clusters of small, red, itchy pimples appear on or around the sex organs. Most often they show up on the soft, moist folds of the vulva at the entry to the girl's vagina, or on the skin of the boy's penis. But they can also appear on the insides of the thighs, on the buttocks, or anywhere else in the area where sexual contact might have occurred.

For a few hours these pimples are just itchy. But soon they begin to ache and burn. Then, within a day or so, the pimples change into painful clusters of fluid-filled blisters called *vesicles*. When these blisters break, they leave raw painful open sores.

At this point the infection is extremely contagious or "spreadable." This is because the open sores are teeming with new virus particles. Doctors would say that the infected person is "shedding virus." This means that the infection can easily be passed from one person to another at this time by sexual contact.

This first or *primary* infection will last for about two weeks. Then the blisters and sores begin to heal. About three or four weeks from the beginning of the primary infection, the sores will be gone, and the active virus will also be gone from the skin. The infected person will then no longer pass the infection on to someone else during sex—until or unless the sores recur.

RECURRING INFECTION

If that primary stage were all there were to it, genital herpes might just be a big nuisance. But just because the primary infection heals doesn't mean that the infection is over. Some lucky people—about 10 or 15 percent—never have any further trouble with genital herpes after that first attack. But most people do. The HSV2 virus is temporarily gone from the skin, but it isn't gone from the body.

From the moment the HSV2 virus first invades the skin cells, the body's immune system starts making special antibodies to fight it off. But the virus isn't destroyed. It just runs and hides in nearby nerve cells, where the antibodies can't get at it. There it can stay "in hiding" for weeks or months, and then come back to cause another or *recurrent* infection. Some people have just one or two recurrent attacks. But others may have them over and over, several times a year. This can go on for years, whether the person is having sex or not. It's the same old infection, coming back again and again.

Recurrent attacks may not be quite as severe as the first one. The blisters appear again, usually in about the same places. They may not hurt as much, and they often don't last as long—perhaps only a few days before healing. But these recurrent sores are the same as the first ones in one important way: they are shedding viruses again, so the infection can again spread to others by sexual contact while the viruses are present.

SPECIAL PROBLEMS
WITH GENITAL HERPES

Genital herpes is not usually a deadly or damaging disease. It doesn't spread to other parts of the body. It doesn't attack a woman's tubes, as gonorrhea or chlamydia can do, nor destroy other organs, as syphilis can. For most people it is just a painful nuisance that comes back again and again and interferes seriously with their sex lives. But there are special cases in which it can be dangerous.

For example, if a pregnant woman has active genital herpes at the time her baby is due to be born, there is a chance the baby may contract the virus at the time of birth. Since the baby's immune system isn't very strong at that time, the child may develop a very severe infection—and some babies have died from this. For this reason, a pregnant woman with genital herpes must be observed very closely as delivery time nears. If her infection recurs and becomes active at the wrong time, it may be necessary for her to have the baby by an operation called *cesarean section,* so that the baby doesn't contact the virus in the mother's vagina.

There is one other possible problem that scientists are investigating today. Doctors suspect that the HSV2 virus may make it easier for a woman to develop cancer

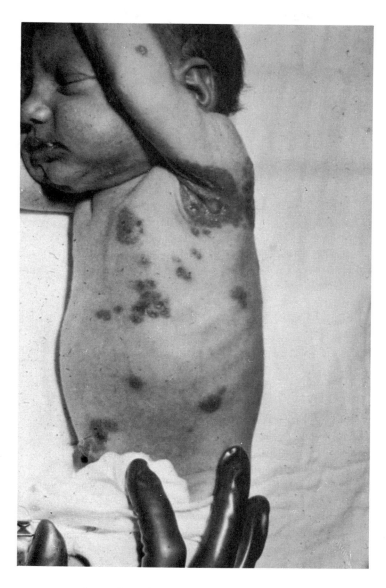

An infant born to a woman infected with active genital herpes. The baby contracted the virus from its mother.

of the cervix later. This has not yet been proven. But we know that this kind of cancer often appears especially early in women who started having sex at an early age, or with many different partners, thus exposing them to genital herpes. Fortunately, a lab test called a *Pap smear* can detect the cancer very early, when it is still completely curable. Any young woman who has genital herpes should have regular Pap smears to detect any sign of this cancer. (There are other sexually transmitted viruses that may also play a role in the early development of this cancer. See the section on *papilloma virus infections* in chapter 8.)

TREATING GENITAL HERPES

Until about ten years ago there was no good way to treat this disease. Once you were infected, you were infected, and there was nothing you could do about it. Then a drug called acyclovir was discovered. This was one of the first so-called *antiviral* drugs to be discovered—drugs that could interfere in some way with the reproduction and spread of certain viruses, somewhat the same as antibiotic drugs like penicillin or tetracycline interfere with the growth of many bacteria. Acyclovir didn't *kill* viruses, so it couldn't *cure* virus diseases. But it *did* seem to prevent the HSV2 virus from reproducing itself in cells grown in the laboratory. When this drug was prepared in an ointment and tested on humans with active genital herpes lesions, these sores and blisters would often heal and become virus-free several days sooner than usual. Later, that same drug was given by mouth in pill form to people with severe, recurrent attacks of genital herpes. It was found, in many cases, to reduce the number and frequency of recurrent attacks very significantly. And those recurrent attacks that did occur tended to be shorter and less painful.

Today, acyclovir in either the ointment or pill form,

or both, has become standard treatment for genital herpes. The drug has to be ordered or *prescribed* by a doctor. It doesn't kill the virus or cure the disease, but for many people it shortens the duration of the primary infection and reduces the frequency and painfulness of recurrent attacks. In short, it makes genital herpes a little easier to live with. Today other antivirus drugs are also under study in hopes that a real cure for genital herpes may someday be found. Scientists are also searching for a vaccine that might protect people from getting the infection in the first place. But so far, acyclovir is the best treatment there is.

PREVENTING
GENITAL HERPES

Obviously, genital herpes is an extremely disagreeable infection to catch. Since it isn't curable, and doesn't go away once you've caught it, *preventing* it makes far more sense than taking the risk of catching it. In chapter 9 we'll talk about the commonsense steps that *anybody* can take to keep from getting *any* kind of sexually transmitted disease. But since prevention is the *only* good answer to genital herpes, we need to preview some of those preventive steps right here.

1. *Saying no to sex* is the safest, surest way there is to keep from getting genital herpes. If you decide to say no to sex for the time being, you won't get this infection. (Forget anything you may have heard about getting it from a toilet seat. It's *possible,* but the real truth is that that's not how people get genital herpes—having sex with an infected person *is.*)

2. If you do have sex, the fewer partners you have the less risk you run of catching the infection. Having sex with just one other person—someone you're sure isn't infected—is the second best way to keep from getting infected yourself. This is just common sense.

3. If you do have sex, *talk* with your partner about genital herpes *before you have sex*. Why talk about it? Because most people who have genital herpes *know* they have it. After all, the symptoms are hard to miss. Even if a person doesn't know for sure what's *causing* certain symptoms, he or she knows that *something* is wrong. There's no excuse for hiding it. Remember that the infection is usually spread only when one or the other partner has an *active* primary infection, or an *active* recurrence *right then* or *very recently*—but unfortunately some persons without symptoms can shed the virus, too. If there's *any* possibility that either you or your partner might have active genital herpes, or might just be recovering from an active episode, then you should postpone sex until a doctor can determine what's going on.

4. If you do have sex, be sure to use a latex rubber condom (sometimes called a "rubber" or a "safety") to protect yourself. If you're a girl, insist that the boy use one. *The genital herpes virus cannot get through this kind of condom.* So using a condom whenever you have sex—and using it *properly*—will protect you from this infection. We'll talk about some simple rules for using condoms properly in chapter 9.

There is one other special factor to consider about transmission of this STD. As the disease has become more widely recognized, a large number of people have discovered that they are infected, and are baffled and angry about it. They can't understand how this could have happened to them, since many of them have never been sexually promiscuous. In fact, many had *never* had sex with anyone but one single partner in their whole life. So where did these infections come from?

Part of the answer lies in the nature of the herpes simplex viruses themselves, and part in changing sexual practices. Although genital herpes is usually caused by the herpes simplex virus #2 (HSV2) and spread by gen-

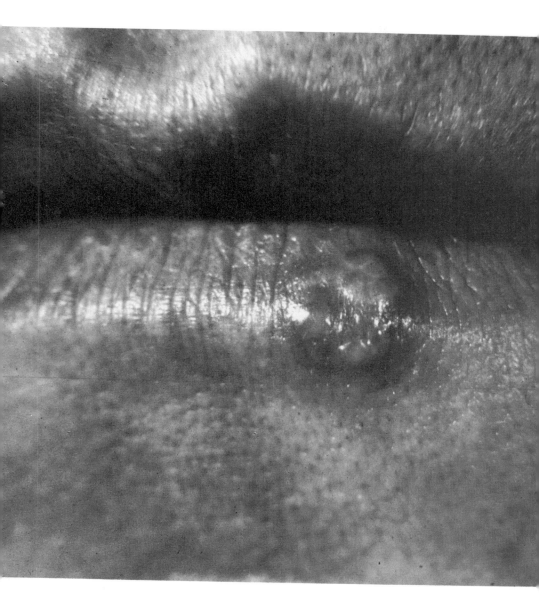

A "cold sore" caused by the
herpes simplex virus

ital contact between partners, the disease can also be caused by the herpes simplex #1 (HSV1), which usually causes cold sores around the mouth or lips. Cold sores are not generally considered sexually transmitted infections, but in modern times many couples engage in oral sex stimulation as a part of their normal sexual practice. This means that a person with an active cold sore on his or her lip can easily transmit HSV1 to a partner's genitals, with a resulting genital herpes infection, and the mystery of "Where did it come from?" is solved. For this reason, to prevent spread of the infection, people should avoid oral sex anytime that an active cold sore is present—and be warned in advance about this possible mode of transmission.

Genital herpes is certainly a thoroughly disagreeable infection, but at least, even if you become infected, you can live with it. Unfortunately, two other virus-caused sexually transmitted diseases—AIDS and hepatitis B—kill people. In the next chapter we'll check some basic facts that you need to know about these deadly diseases.

7
HIV DISEASE (AIDS) AND HEPATITIS B

Any STD can mean trouble for the person who is infected. But of all the sexually transmitted diseases we know of, **HIV disease (AIDS)** is by far the worst, and **hepatitis B** is not far behind. Both these diseases kill people. HIV disease is one of the most deadly diseases ever known. What is more, infection with the virus that causes HIV disease is spreading rapidly. That virus has become a terrible threat to everybody, including any young people who are sexually active today—not just to male homosexuals, or intravenous drug users, or other persons in certain small "high-risk" groups, as some people would like to imagine. The fact is that *everybody* is at risk today, and that risk is not going to diminish in the future unless every sexually active person does what is necessary to diminish the risk for himself or herself.

For this reason, everybody needs to know some hard facts about infection with the Human Immunodeficiency Virus (HIV) and the *syndrome* or pattern of symptoms known as AIDS that it causes, as well as about hepatitis B. What are these infections? What can they do to you? How are they spread from person to person? And above all, how can you protect yourself from them?

A NEW AND DEADLY VIRUS

Just about everybody has heard of AIDS by now, but you may not be so familiar with the term "HIV disease," so let's get that straightened out to begin with. There is a virus known as the **Human Immunodeficiency Virus**, or HIV, which can infect human beings. When a person has been infected with HIV, the virus doesn't go away—the infected person has HIV disease, then and there, and from then on. This virus infection may not cause any symptoms for a long time, maybe not for months or years, but from the moment of infection on, HIV is attacking and slowly destroying the victim's immune protective system.

At some point, the immune system becomes so weakened by this virus that a variety of symptoms begin to appear. This collection of end-stage symptoms, which doctors call a *syndrome,* is referred to as the Acquired Immune Deficiency Syndrome, or AIDS. They represent a late and usually fatal stage of HIV disease. The underlying disease is the HIV infection, but not everyone who is infected with HIV automatically has AIDS. Only those in whom late-stage symptoms have begun to appear are said to have AIDS.

Unlike other STDs, which have been around for many years, HIV disease is a comparative newcomer. Health experts now believe that a few people here and there were dying of AIDS—without knowing it—as early as 1952 or even before. But the disease was not recognized as a distinct, separate killer until about 1978, and its spread did not reach *epidemic* proportions in the United States until 1981. In that year, approximately 150 cases of AIDS were diagnosed, and some 30 people died from HIV disease.

76

By July of 1990—just nine years later—more than 143,286 cases of AIDS had been reported in the United States alone, and over 87,644 of those people had died from the disease. This means that a total of 61 percent of all persons in the United States ever diagnosed with full-blown AIDS—more than six out of every ten—have already died.* Multitudes of other cases and deaths had occurred worldwide. Nor is the epidemic slowing down. In fact, according to projections by the Centers for Disease Control (CDC) in Atlanta, Georgia—our national public health authority on AIDS—by the end of 1993, the total number of AIDS cases in the United States will be between 390,000 and 480,000, with a cumulative death toll of between 285,000 and 340,000. For 1993 *alone* the estimates are between 150,000 and 252,000 new cases diagnosed.

The real tragedy is that many of these new cases of AIDS projected in the future will occur in people who are *already* infected with HIV *right now—today*—and just haven't developed any symptoms yet. Scientists believe that more than 1.5 *million* people in this country may already be infected with HIV without yet being sick from it. And new people—including teenagers and young people—are being infected with it every day.

THE VIRUS INVADERS

To understand what the Human Immunodeficiency Virus is and how it does its damage, we need to review some simple, basic facts about viruses in general.

Viruses are the tiniest of all the disease-causing germs, so very small they can only be seen under a pow-

---

* U.S. Public Health Service, Centers for Disease Control, Atlanta, Ga., multiple reports. See also current (8/23/1990) AIDS statistics bulletin supplied by Yakima/Kittitas County (Washington) Public Health Department.

erful electron microscope. Viruses have been around on earth for a long, long time—probably longer than even the first living cells. And compared to a living cell, a virus is extremely simple indeed. It is nothing more than a molecule of DNA (deoxyribonucleic acid) or RNA (ribonucleic acid) wrapped up in a protein envelope. DNA is the familiar double-helix molecule that makes up the *genes* in living cells—the hereditary material that dictates the structure and function of every life form. RNA is essentially just a small segment of DNA which is responsible for the manufacture of all cellular and viral proteins. When living cells divide, the packets of DNA or RNA they contain also divide, so that each daughter cell contains a replica of the hereditary material in the parent cell. Since virus particles normally have no living cells surrounding them, they have been described quite accurately as tiny fragments of hereditary material on the loose.

Viruses are very different from living cells. They don't carry on any life processes of their own. They don't need any food. They don't need any water, or any other solvent. They don't need oxygen, or any other atmospheric gas to survive. In fact, there are only two things they *do* need. They need the *right temperature*—if it gets too cold or too hot, their protein coating will be destroyed. And they need freedom from noxious chemicals, such as formaldehyde, which can also destroy their protein coating.

As long as those conditions are met, viruses don't actually need to do *anything*—they can just sit there forever. Indeed, viruses *can't* do anything by themselves; they can't grow, they can't reproduce themselves, they can't do anything at all—*until they get inside a living cell somewhere.*

When viruses do get inside a human body—from the air, from respiratory droplets, from sexual contact— they attach themselves to little molecular sockets called *receptors* on the surface of certain "host" cells. Once latched on, they squirt their DNA or RNA into the host cells. It is from that point on, inside the host cell, that the virus takes charge of things. Its DNA or RNA attaches itself to the cell's own DNA and changes its whole purpose. Suddenly the cell's normal functions are overpowered, and the virus forces the cell to start making more virus particles. It doesn't take long. In some cases a single invading virus particle can force its host cell to make 200 virus particle replicas in as little as 25 minutes. In most cases, this destroys the cell. The cell bursts apart, and hundreds of new virus particles pour out into the bloodstream and go on to find more host cells. In those cells, the process is repeated, and soon *millions* of virus particles are flooding the bloodstream. This condition is called a *viremia*—"viruses in the bloodstream."

FIGHTING THE INVADERS

If viruses can invade human bodies in this manner and force our bodies' cells to make so many more virus particles so very quickly, with the host cells dying right and left in the process, why haven't we all died of virus infections long since?

The answer is fascinating: we are normally protected by our human immune system—a built-in defense system against virus invaders. This system of cells and chemicals, spread all over the body, contains a variety of special white blood cells that can detect virus particles as "foreign invaders" almost as soon as they enter the body, and mount a furious attack to destroy them. Other white blood cells are transformed into "antibody factories" which manufacture tailor-made protein molecules (antibodies) to aid in the destruction of the viruses.

Ever since this complex immune system evolved millions of years ago, it has been the human body's major defense against devastating virus infections. And

79

in most cases the immune system wins the battle, and the virus invaders are destroyed. Even in the case of an especially deadly virus infection such as smallpox, a disease that once swept through whole populations in vast epidemics, only 20 or 30 percent of the victims died. The rest were saved by their immune systems, and recovered. And once recovered, those people never again had another case of smallpox—they were permanently *immune* to new attacks of the virus.

Then HIV, the Human Immunodeficiency Virus, came along, and the story was very different.

When a person is infected by HIV, the invading virus seeks out certain white blood cells called *lymphocytes* and *macrophages* as their favorite "host cells." As it happens, these are the very cells the body counts on the most to fight down virus invaders—the key cells of the human immune system itself. During HIV infection, HIV particles seek out these cells and shoulder their way inside them. There the virus takes command of these cells and forces them to begin making HIV particles, killing those vital cells in the process, while millions of new virus particles are released into the bloodstream. From there they go on to infect more of these vital cells. This is HIV disease.

Gradually, more and more of these immune system cells are killed, and more and more HIV particles are made. And very slowly, the immune system's function is destroyed in the process. All this may take as long as three or four or even ten years or more without any actual symptoms appearing. But meanwhile, all those HIV particles are piling up in the bloodstream and in other body fluids, particularly in the man's **semen** (the fluid which he ejaculates during sex) and in the woman's vaginal secretions. And all this time the infected person can pass the deadly virus on to infect others during sexual contact, or by sharing dirty intravenous drug needles which have been contaminated with virus-infested blood.

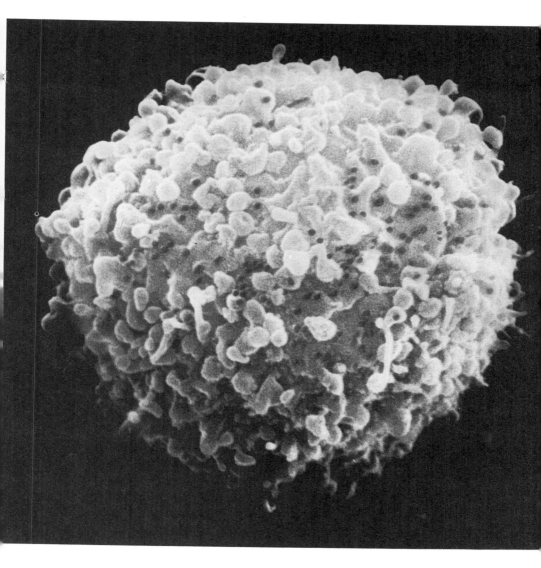

A T-lymphocyte cell infected with the Human Immunodeficiency Virus (HIV). An infected cell typically has a lumpy appearance with irregularly rounded protrusions.

TESTING FOR HIV

There may be no sign of infection for months or even years after the virus gets into the body. But there *is* a way to tell that the virus is there, just the same. Soon after HIV first invades the body, antibodies against the virus begin appearing. These antibodies don't seem to kill the invading germs, but they hold them in check for a while. Meanwhile, by doing special blood tests, laboratories can detect the antibodies in the person's bloodstream. If the antibodies are there, it means the person is already infected with HIV, even though no symptoms of sickness caused by HIV disease have appeared. And if HIV is there in a person's body, that person can pass it on to others, whether he or she seems to be sick or not.

Nobody can say exactly how long it will take a person to become *sick* from HIV disease, once he or she is infected. Some people start getting sick within a few months. Others don't get sick for years. Maybe some never *will* get sick—nobody yet knows for sure, and nobody knows who will ultimately get sick and who won't. So far, about 90 percent of the people known to be infected with HIV seem to get sick from it sooner or later. Some experts believe that virtually *everybody* infected with the virus will begin to have the end-stage symptoms *sometime,* assuming they live long enough.

These end-stage symptoms occur when the HIV disease has finally beaten the immune system down to the ground, and it begins to fall apart and can't function anymore. As we have seen, the person developing these symptoms is said to have AIDS. And once those symptoms begin, there is never any recovery—the syndrome sooner or later proves fatal.

SYMPTOMS OF AIDS

The end-stage symptoms of HIV disease that mark the beginning of AIDS can vary a great deal from person to person. Some infected people start having nausea, vomiting, and extreme weight loss, or have high fevers and sweating at night. Others develop swollen glands all over the body.

Still others have more dangerous symptoms. There are many diseases that normal people never get because their immune systems successfully fight them down before they can really get started. But these diseases become deadly threats to people with AIDS who have lost their immune protection. Many AIDS patients, for example, come down with a deadly lung infection caused by a germ called *Pneumocystis carinii*. This pneumonia is very hard to treat and control with antibiotics, and tends to keep coming back even after it has been treated. Others develop an unusual kind of cancer of blood vessels in the skin called *Kaposi's sarcoma*, seldom seen in normal people. Various other infections caused by fungi, protozoans, or herpes viruses torment these people. These infections are called **opportunistic infections** because they only appear when they have a special opportunity because the person's damaged immune system can't fight them off adequately. And many AIDS victims have another kind of problem, too. The virus may attack nerve cells as well as lymphocytes, causing severe problems with the way the brain and nervous system work.

These symptoms may vary from person to person, but the final deadly nature of this syndrome is the same for everyone. Before a treatment was discovered, patients who developed the symptoms of AIDS just got sicker and sicker and finally died, usually within about two years. Fortunately, within the last few years, at least one antiviral drug has been proven to help slow the progress of the disease. This drug, known as *zidovudine* or AZT, interferes with the production of new HIV particles. The drug has been found to extend the lives of AIDS patients and help them recover enough to live more normally for a while. Unfortunately, zidovudine is very toxic, so that many people with AIDS can't take it for very long.

Several other drugs now under study show great promise for the future; some may help fight down the virus just as effectively as zidovudine does, or in different ways than zidovudine does, and be less poisonous in themselves. But none of these medicines can *cure* HIV infection, and so far no vaccine has been perfected to protect people from the infection. Your only real protection is *not to become infected in the first place*. But to protect yourself, you need to know how the infection is spread.

HOW HIV IS SPREAD

When a person is infected by HIV, whether any symptoms have appeared or not, that person can pass the virus on to others. As we have seen, the viruses are present in great numbers in the infected person's blood, in the man's semen, or the woman's vaginal secretions. Contact with these fluids spread HIV disease. In fact, HIV experts believe that HIV disease is spread from person to person in just four main ways:

1. *You can get an HIV infection by having sex with an infected person.* This is the main route of infection for people who don't inject illegal drugs. *Any sex contact with an infected person is hazardous.*

Here we must clear up a mistaken idea many people have about HIV disease. Because so many of the first AIDS victims were male homosexuals (men who have sex with men), many people still think that HIV disease is a "homosexual disease." They think that heterosexual people (those who have only male-female sex) are safe from infection. This is simply not true. *Anyone* infected with HIV can pass it on to *anyone* else, male or female, during sex. Many people in this country have already caught the infection from male-female sexual contact,

84

and in Africa and parts of Europe male-female sex is the main route of infection. In other words, HIV infection is a *sexually transmitted disease.* And like any other STD, it can be passed on through *any* sexual contact with an infected person, homosexual or heterosexual.

2. You can acquire an HIV infection by injecting drugs with dirty needles contaminated with the virus-infested blood of infected people. This is one of the most common ways that HIV disease is transmitted in places like New York City, where there are large numbers of illegal drug users.

3. You can get an HIV infection by contact with *any* HIV-contaminated blood or blood products. Before 1985, some people were infected with HIV from ordinary transfusions of blood donated by infected people. Many of them were innocent people with a blood disease known as *hemophilia* who had to have frequent transfusions to stay alive. A number of school-age children got HIV disease this way. Since 1985 all donated blood is tested for HIV antibodies before it is used for transfusion, so this source of infection is very much reduced.

4. Finally, a woman infected with HIV can pass the virus on to infect her unborn baby. This accounts for hundreds of cases of HIV disease in newborn babies.

It's important to know how HIV is passed on from person to person. But it's also important to know how it *isn't* passed on. For instance, it *isn't* passed on by casual contact with an infected person in the classroom or on the playground. It *isn't* passed on by sneezing or coughing or noseblowing the way a cold or flu virus might be. And it *isn't* passed on by using the same toilet facilities. The ordinary person going to school or work just doesn't have to worry about HIV infection from casual contact. Basically, there are just two things you *do* have to worry about: catching an HIV infection from dirty drug-injecting equipment, or from sexual contact.

85

An AIDS Hotline for Kids poster
appeals to people not to discriminate
against children with AIDS.

GUARDING AGAINST HIV INFECTION, HIV DISEASE, AND AIDS

Once you know how HIV disease is spread, it's easy to see how you can protect yourself from catching it.

For most young people, it's easy to avoid infected drug-injecting equipment. The rules are simple. *If you don't use illegal injectable drugs, never start. If you do use them, stop—for your life's sake.* And never use a needle for *anything* if somebody else has used it for *anything*—not even picking out a splinter.

The connection between HIV infection and dirty injection equipment is perfectly clear. Thousands of people have already developed and died from AIDS this way. But nobody *has* to use illegal injectable drugs, and it's possible for anyone using them to stop. If you are using, *get help.* Talk to somebody—a doctor, a trusted counselor, your parents, a minister, *anybody you can trust*—to help you get out of a drug scene that could easily be deadly.

The risk of getting HIV infection from sexual contact is harder to deal with. But there are things you can do to protect yourself here, too. These same things will help protect you from *any* sexually transmitted disease, not just HIV disease alone. We'll talk about these things in detail in chapter 9. But while we are talking about HIV disease, we should consider another dangerous virus-caused STD that is spread in much the same way that HIV infection is spread.

HEPATITIS B ("SERUM HEPATITIS")

This virus infection has been around much longer than HIV and AIDS, and hepatitis B infection shares some common ground with HIV infection. This particular virus attacks and destroys cells in the liver. In some cases it causes an acute infection marked by a high fever, severe pain in the abdomen over the liver, generalized weakness, loss of appetite, nausea and vomiting, and a marked yellowish coloring of the skin and the whites of the eyes known as *jaundice*. The urine turns dark brown and the stools become almost white. In other cases, there may be very few symptoms, and little hint that the infection is present until the jaundice appears. In either case, it's a very dangerous infection—one out of ten victims die from severe liver damage during the acute attack. For those who don't die, recovery can take weeks or months, and about three out of ten of those survivors become lifelong *carriers* of the virus—that is, they continue to carry the live virus in their blood and other body fluids, so they can pass the infection on to others even after they seem to have recovered.

For a long while doctors thought that the hepatitis B virus was only spread among drug users who shared dirty injection equipment. But now we know that infected people also shed live viruses from moist body surfaces such as the sex organs. This means that hepatitis B is a sexually transmitted disease that can be passed on by sexual contact.

Hepatitis B was, and still is, very common among the same special high-risk groups who are most vulnerable to HIV infection—male homosexuals and IV drug users. But it is becoming more and more widespread among heterosexual people due to sexual transmission. In 1989 more than 23,000 new cases were reported in that single year, according to the Centers for Disease Control, in spite of the fact that an effective protective vaccine has been available since 1982. So far there is no cure for hepatitis B, nor any drug effective for controlling it, but more widespread use of the vaccine, especially to protect people at special risk (hospital workers, for example, or family members of an infected person, or persons who use illegal IV drugs) could reduce the incidence of the disease substantially.

As with HIV infection, the best protection against hepatitis B is prevention of the infection in the first place. We'll discuss some measures you can take to protect yourself against HIV disease, hepatitis B, or any other sexually transmitted disease, in chapter 9. But first we should complete the roster of sexually transmitted diseases with some information about a few other STDs that you hardly ever hear mentioned at all.

⑧
STDs THAT NOBODY TALKS ABOUT

Many of the STDs we've been discussing are at least reasonably familiar to most people. People have heard of them, and people talk about them to some extent. Certainly HIV disease and the syndrome it causes, AIDS, is the most widely and publicly discussed sexually transmitted disease in all history. The fact that gonorrhea has so many different common or "street" nicknames tells us that the disease is very familiar and gets talked about a lot, and discussions about chlamydia infections are appearing all over in popular magazines.

There are, however, a few sexually transmitted diseases—or closely related conditions—that nobody talks about at all. For one reason, many people just don't recognize these things as STDs in the first place, even though they often are. In addition, they aren't very *pleasant* conditions to talk about. People prefer not even to think about them. Yet all of them are quite common, and one of them, at least, has recently been recognized to be epidemic among teenagers today, and quite dangerous as a contributor to cancer of the sex organs. Among these diseases are **genital warts** (papilloma virus infections), **pediculosis** infestations (crab lice), and **scabies.**

GENITAL WARTS

These unpleasant wartlike growths typically develop and enlarge in the genital and rectal areas of both males and females. They cluster around the rectum, at the entrance to the urine tube, or along the folds of the woman's vulva, or on the man's scrotum or penis. Doctors sometimes speak of them as *condylomata acuminatum.* These gray-colored warty affairs may be small and single, but often enlarge rapidly and bunch together in large, moist, cauliflower-like growths. Sometimes they don't cause any symptoms at all. At other times they may cause itching, burning, pain or soreness, and occasionally bleeding. A few years ago they were most common in people twenty to twenty-four years of age, with women more often affected than men—but now they are turning up more and more frequently among sexually active teens. They often appear along with other STDs such as gonorrhea or chlamydia infections, and as one might expect, they are particularly prevalent in people who have many different sex partners.

Genital warts are caused by various members of a family of viruses known as **human papilloma viruses** or **HPVs.** (A "papilloma" is just a wart, in medical terms.) There are at least thirty different viruses in this family, and they produce a wide variety of different warts, including the ordinary lumpy warts people get on their fingers, the flat warts that appear on the face, and the painful plantar warts that may grow on the soles of the feet, as well as genital warts.

Genital warts are caused by a number of these

HPVs, especially HPV-6 and HPV-11. Unlike most other STD infections, after exposure these warts often take several weeks or months to develop. Sometimes they appear one at a time, or in small groups. At other times, there may be a sudden "flowering" of them. Obviously, this slow, irregular development of genital warts can make it hard to be sure when or with whom the exposure occurred, if the person has had more than one sex partner—yet as we will see, this can be very important to determine, if possible, especially among sexually active teenagers.

Since there are no good antiviral drugs to eradicate genital warts, they are usually best treated by applying various destructive agents to the surface of the warts themselves. One such agent is *podophyllin*, a caustic resin derived from the roots of certain plants. The podophyllin solution is carefully applied to the individual warts, and then washed off three or four hours later, since it is extremely irritating to adjacent skin. The warts are effectively "burned off" or dessicated by this substance. Treatment is repeated a week or so later to remove any remaining warts. A third treatment a month later will help control any recurrent lesions. Usually the doctor treating genital warts will also look for evidence of any other STDs that may be present at the same time, and a serological test for syphilis is also recommended.

More recently, other less irritating treatments have been tried. Sometimes the warts can be painlessly frozen and destroyed with liquid nitrogen, or burned off with an electric needle or laser beam, or be surgically removed, all under local anesthesia. Recent studies have shown that injection of the warts-affected areas with *interferon alpha-2b*, a natural immune system product, can also help destroy the warts. Unfortunately, that treatment can cause such general side effects as fever, chills, or muscle aching, so it is used mainly to treat warts that have resisted other treatment.

THE PAPILLOMA VIRUS DANGER

For years HPV infections, including genital warts, were considered more of a distasteful nuisance than any serious threat to health. But recent discoveries have changed that picture. The HPVs not only cause warts around the genital regions, but also infect the woman's vaginal lining and the cells on the surface of the cervix, the mouth of the uterus. Doctors now recognize a strong connection between these HPV infections in women and the early development of cancers of the female genitals, particularly cancer of the cervix. Apparently, the earlier in her life that a girl is exposed and develops these papilloma virus infections, the greater the risk that she will develop such cancers at an early age. Nobody knows whether the HPVs are actually the *direct* cause of the cancers, or whether they are merely one contributing factor. What *is* known is that girls with these HPV infections are being discovered to have cancer of the vulva or cervix as early as sixteen or seventeen years of age.

In practical terms, this means two things. First, it means that genital warts need to be taken very seriously. They must be discovered and treated just as soon as they appear—and this can be tough, because most teen girls are very reluctant to go see a doctor about something like this, especially if there are very few, if any, symptoms involved. (Obviously, if you are having serious abdominal pain from pelvic inflammatory disease, or PID, you're likely to seek medical help quickly, but if you've just got a few warts that itch a little bit, you might decide not to go unless you understood the danger.) What's more, not only should the woman be treated, but her partner or partners should be examined and treated too, since reinfection is a real problem here, and the infections have to be *stopped*.

Second, it means that any girl who has started having sex early, or with many partners, should also start having Pap tests for the early detection of cancer of the cervix. The Pap test is named after its inventor, Dr. George Papanicolaou, a Greek-born American doctor. It is simple, painless, and quite inexpensive. For this test, fluid from the vagina and cells scraped from the cervix are examined under a microscope in search of cells that show early cancerlike changes. It can detect cancer of the cervix as much as five to ten years before any symptoms appear, so that in most cases a cancer can be quickly and completely cured. Before the Pap test, cancer of the cervix was a major killer of women. With early detection, there is no reason today for *any* woman to die of this cancer.

Most doctors feel that any girl who has become sexually active in her teens should start having Pap tests at once, repeated at least once a year, for her own protection. And this is especially true when genital warts are found to be present, because of the increased risk of early cancer of the cervix.

The best protection against genital wart infections involves the same safeguards that work against any other STD, especially the use of a condom to protect against direct skin-to-skin contact with an infected person. We'll talk about those "safe-sex" safeguards more in the next chapter.

PEDICULOSIS

Technically, this problem—infestation with pubic lice or so-called crab lice or "crabs"—isn't a sexually transmitted disease at all. It can occur anytime a person has close bodily contact with an infested person, or even uses the same bedclothes. These lice tend to appear in circumstances of poor hygiene, among people who just don't bathe much, or who live in filthy conditions. The lice particularly like to set up housekeeping on hairy parts of the body other than the scalp—in the area of pubic hair,

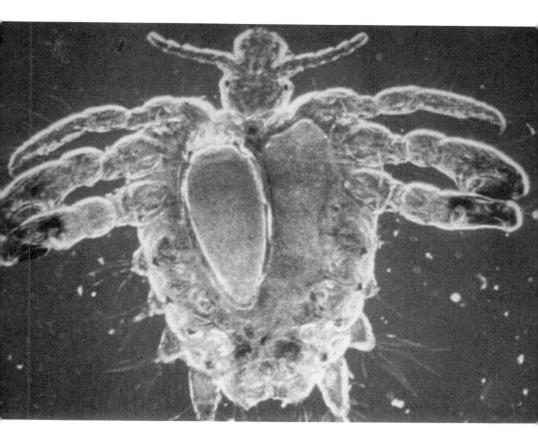

The female crab louse, the tiny organism
that causes pediculosis or "crabs"

around the rectum, or in unshaven underarm areas. They're easy enough to detect—they're about $\frac{1}{16}$th of an inch long, lay their nits, or eggs, on the hair shafts, and cause itching or irritation when they crawl around. Under a magnifying glass they look like little crabs, hence their name. (A different kind of louse, the head louse, prefers the scalp.) And they very often are transmitted from one person to another during sexual contact.

Pubic lice aren't dangerous—they don't transmit diseases—but they are a thoroughly distasteful nuisance. They can be eliminated by external application of over-the-counter preparations containing pyrethrins and piperonyl butoxide, which work together to kill the lice and nits, followed by vigorous sudsing with soap and rinsing with water. There are a number of products available, including A-200 Pediculocide Gel and Rid Lice Treatment. To prevent reinfestation, all clothing and bedding that might be contaminated should be boiled before reuse after treatment. Since some of the nits may survive the first treatment and hatch into lice, treatment should be repeated in seven to ten days.

SCABIES

This is another parasite infestation which isn't exactly sexually transmitted, but can be passed from person to person by close body contact or use of infested bedding. The parasite is a tiny, almost invisible itch-mite known as *Sarcoptes scabiei*. This little devil burrows under the outer layer of skin to lay its eggs, causing tiny red pinpoint lesions that itch almost unbearably. The major danger here is scratching, which can introduce bacterial infection into the skin, turning an almighty uncomfortable nuisance into a more serious problem. Scabies can often be confused with ringworm-type fungus infections of the skin. Since the two things require totally different

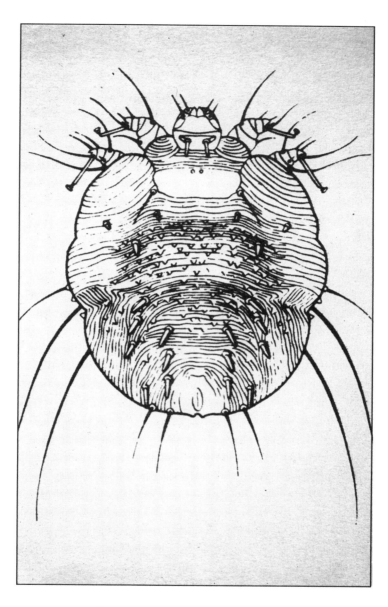

*Another tiny parasite, Sarcoptes scabiei,
causes what is commonly known as scabies.*

treatments, one should have a doctor confirm the diagnosis before treating scabies.

Treatment with preparations containing the insecticide *lindane* in 1 percent concentration (Kwell Cream, etc.) is quick and effective. Since some people have allergic reactions and other side effects from this stuff, it is sold by doctor's prescription only. The cream is applied from the neck down all over the body and left on for eight to ten hours, then thoroughly washed off. One application is usually curative. Again, infested bedclothes and clothing should be boiled after treatment and before reuse to prevent reinfestation.

As we have seen, most STDs (with the notable exceptions of HIV disease and hepatitis B) can be at least controlled, if not cured, if diagnosed and then effectively treated. But treatment of any STD is obviously a matter of locking the barn door after the horse has been stolen. The really smart way for anybody, and especially young people, to deal with STDs is to keep from getting them in the first place. It's perfectly possible to do so, and it's just plain commonsense self-protection in our world today. In the next chapter we'll discuss the simple, effective ways you can protect yourself and minimize the chances of ever getting one of these infections.

⑨
PROTECTING YOURSELF AGAINST STDs

Just reading this book might make you think that almost everybody has trouble with sexually transmitted diseases all the time. Of course that's not true. Many people spend their whole lives without ever once having an STD. People who pick their sexual partners very carefully, after long, close acquaintance, don't often get STDs. Neither do married couples who have sex exclusively with each other. They may worry about having unwanted pregnancies, but not about STDs.

Other people *do* risk getting these infections—some more than others. The ones who run the greatest risk are people who have lots of sexual contact with lots of different people they don't know very well, or with people who are very likely to be infected—casual pickups, or prostitutes, for instance.

Young people run a special risk of getting STDs for two reasons. First, they are just beginning to explore sex, without knowing too much about their partners or even what STDs are all about, and without much experience in judging when to be nervous and cautious. Second, there is already a large number of infected young people out there to catch these diseases from. The plain fact that the number of new cases of sexually transmitted diseases today is increasing faster in young people in their teens than in any other age group is the main reason this book has been written.

Nobody *has* to get these infections. It is perfectly possible to keep from getting them at all, and still enjoy a commonsense and satisfying sex life that fits in with your own needs, beliefs, and principles. And if you do become infected, it is possible—in most cases—to get treatment before you suffer any bad consequences.

How can you protect yourself? Knowing what STDs are, and the problems they can cause, is a big step in the right direction. After that, protecting yourself depends on two main principles: ***living defensively*** and ***getting medical help when you need it.***

LIVING DEFENSIVELY

A soldier on patrol in a jungle or desert War Zone doesn't take any chances that he can possibly avoid. His rifle is loaded, his helmet on, his grenade belt handy, and he is constantly on the alert. He knows that there are lots of people out there who aren't interested in his safety. If he wants protection from danger, he'd better protect himself and his buddies, because nobody else is going to do it for him. This means he has to be ready for anything that might come along, however unpleasant it may be. He believes in *living defensively.*

As far as sexually transmitted diseases are concerned, the world you are living in today is a War Zone. If you catch an STD, *you* are the one in trouble, nobody else. Maybe the person you are having sex with will worry about protecting you, but you'd better not count on it. Like that soldier on patrol, you need to be ready to protect yourself against anything. "Living defensively" simply means arranging your life to protect yourself against these infections as much as is reasonably possible. Living defensively will offer you the *best possible protection* against getting HIV. But it can also protect you from all the other sexually transmitted diseases as well.

Living defensively doesn't mean being totally anti-social, or trying to live locked up in an armored car, guarding yourself from everything and everybody. Nobody wants a life like that. Living defensively *does* mean using plain common sense to protect yourself from obvious dangers. It means *respecting* yourself as a worthwhile person—maybe the most worthwhile person around, as far as you're concerned. It means recognizing that yes, there really *are* dangerous things around out there, and knowing what they are. It means realizing that yes, bad things *can* happen to you, if you don't pay attention—can and very possibly *will* happen, if you just stand around and let them. It means *valuing* yourself enough to live your life the way *you* think is right for you, not the way somebody else may think. And that means exercising some self-control over the way you live, for your very own benefit, and being willing and able, when necessary, to say no when everybody else seems to be saying yes.

Here are some basic clues for living defensively:

1. **Refuse any contact with injectable drugs.** This is especially vital for protection against HIV disease and hepatitis B, two of the nastiest and most dangerous of the STDs we have discussed, so we put it first. We *know* that using dirty drug injection equipment is a major way that HIV infection is spread from person to person. Thousands of people have already become AIDS victims this way. Anybody who injects drugs is just taking a whopping risk. Hepatitis B, another dangerous sexually transmitted virus infection, is also spread this way.

The rules we listed earlier for self-protection are very simple and worth stating again. *If you don't use illegal injectable drugs, never start—not even once just to "try it." If you do use them, stop—for your life's sake. And never, for any reason, use a needle or syringe that somebody else has used.*

As we mentioned earlier, nobody *has* to start using injectable drugs, and those who do can stop if they understand the danger they are in—and care. All kinds of people have done it. Get help from a doctor, a trusted counselor, a parent, a minister, or anybody else you can trust to help you get out of the injectable drug scene if you're in it. And do it *now*. Don't wait.

Sad to say, one of the facts of life today is that there are some people who can't or won't stop using injectable drugs, and who *don't* care. There is a high reservoir of HIV and hepatitis B infection among those people, and they are transmitting the viruses to others by sexual contact as well as by sharing needles. Of course, it isn't injecting the drugs themselves that spreads these infections—it's using the dirty, contaminated needles and injection equipment previously used by somebody else who is infected. Traces of infected blood are in the needle, and the viruses in that blood can survive and remain infectious for hours or days—it's as simple and basic as that. For people close to these people, sharing sex with them can be just as deadly as sharing dirty needles with them. So a second rule for defensive living is, simply, don't have sex with these people.

Finally, there are two ways that even those people can protect themselves if they aren't already infected. Some communities are making needle-exchange programs available. Bring in your dirty needle and trade it for a fresh, sterilized needle. Even more widespread are community "Teach and Bleach" programs. Ordinary kitchen Clorox is a disinfectant that kills both HIV and hepatitis B viruses, and Clorox is very inexpensive in any grocery store. These programs seek to teach and encourage IV drug users to take the moment necessary

102

*A demonstrator in New York advocates
a program that provided drug addicts
with clean, free needles.*

to rinse their dirty needles and syringes or other injection equipment with Clorox and then with clean water after every use. If everybody involved would do this, the terrible danger of the IV drug route of transmission of these diseases could be brought under control. For those people, this simple procedure is indeed "living defensively" in every sense of the word.

Saying no to injectable drugs is, of course, a specific defense against HIV and hepatitis B infection. However, these are not the only dangerous drugs around. You can be trapped just as easily by the use of alcohol, marijuana, cocaine, speed, or other so-called "recreational" drugs. But the trap is more subtle. *Any* of these drugs can cloud your mind and interfere with your reason and common sense. They can block your capacity to use preventive measures, or make you indifferent to real dangers. They can fool you into thinking it can't happen to you. A surgeon doesn't get drunk or high on marijuana before doing a heart transplant operation. He needs all his mental sharpness going for him. So do you.

For more general defensive-living tips to guard against *all* sexually transmitted diseases, consider the following rules:

2. **Decide to postpone sex.** There are obviously lots of reasons why having sex is pleasant and desirable. Sexual urges are basic and powerful natural driving forces in everybody's life. But sexually transmitted diseases are one very big reason why having sex may *not* be such a pleasant and desirable idea, at least for the time being. One of the facts of life is that young people who decide to postpone sex, at least for the time being, don't have to worry about contracting STDs.

There are many other reasons today to consider postponing sex for a while. You already know some of them. These could include your parents' concerns for you, your own religious upbringing, or your community's attitudes toward sex and marriage. Maybe the most important reason is your own sense of self-esteem and self-respect—of being your own person and making your own decisions.

Lots of young people aren't really all that eager to start having sex right away anyway. They sense that starting a sex relationship with somebody inevitably involves very strong emotions, and such relationships can end up being extremely painful and hurtful unless some real long-term love and commitment are involved, too. They realize that having sex isn't just a carefree game— it involves some serious rules and consequences. But even young people who feel cautious about starting sex relations may at the same time feel pressured into having sex right away by those around them. When you consider that STDs are a real threat, and that saying no to sex is the surest way to protect yourself against them— and a lot of other headaches too—this knowledge may help you make (and stick to) a decision that you'd just as soon make anyway.

3. If you do have sex, **keep self-protection in mind.** First, try to keep it a *monogamous* or "one-person" relationship. It's just common sense that the more different sex partners you have, the greater your risk of coming in contact with the Human Immunodeficiency Virus or other STDs. The fewer sex partners you have, the smaller the risk. And the better you know your sex partner, the less the risk. Best of all is to pick one partner you know hasn't had all kinds of sex contacts previously, and then keep the sex relationship between you just as much of a "one-person only" matter as you possibly can.

When it comes to deciding on a sex partner, there's another defensive-living factor to bear in mind: it's a fact of life that you can't always take everything that someone says at face value. People tend to lie about their past and present sexual activities. In a recent survey of sexually active college students in California, published in a major medical journal,* researchers asked both males and females questions about how they went about deciding to have sex with somebody or not. Quite a number of the students said that they had talked with prospective partners about their past sexual histories. As one girl put it, "As far as AIDS is concerned, if you're going to go to bed with a guy, you're not just going to bed with *him,* you're going to bed with everybody else he's ever slept with as well." You might think that this kind of before-sex exploration is a very good idea, and it *is*—but don't count too heavily on the answers you receive. This survey found that about 75 percent of the men interviewed, and some 50 percent of the women, admitted that they had lied to prospective sex partners because they were afraid that telling the bald truth might have spoiled their chances for sex. Let a word to the wise be sufficient. The best answer to this problem is that a fairly lengthy and intimate *non*sexual relationship with a person before actually having sex is probably a better guide to his or her actual sexual history than any amount of impulse-driven, under-the-gun, now-or-never conversation. Caution is the word.

4. No matter how well you know your partner, **use a condom and a spermicidal jelly or foam whenever you have sex.****

A **condom** (sometimes called a "rubber" or "safety") is a tube of very thin latex rubber, closed at one end, which is rolled down over the boy's erect penis before he starts having sex. The condom prevents *actual di-*

---

* V. M. Mays and S. D. Cochran, "Sex Lies, and HIV," *The New England Journal of Medicine* 322, no. 11 (March 15, 1990): 774.

** Obviously, this does not apply to couples having sex in marriage, or when planning for children is a part of the equation—although many such couples do use the condom-and-foam combination as one means of birth control. For more information about effective birth control methods, *see* Alan E. Nourse, M.D., *Birth Control* (New York: Franklin Watts, 1988).

rect contact between penis and vulva or vagina during sex. Scientists have shown that even a germ as tiny as HIV cannot get through an ordinary latex rubber condom. Neither can the germs that cause gonorrhea, syphilis, genital herpes, or other STDs. (The so-called "natural" or sheep-gut condoms do *not* offer this protection, so forget about them.)

A **spermicide** is a jelly or foam that contains a chemical called *nonoxynol-9*. This chemical kills sperm cells on contact. It also kills *all* STD germs, if you use enough of it. So using a spermicide along with a condom adds extra protection against STD germs.

For this condom-and-spermicide combination to really protect you against STDs, you have to use it correctly. Here are some commonsense rules to follow:*

a. Use a condom *every single time* you have sex.

b. The boy should put on the condom as soon as his penis is erect, before he has *any* contact with the girl's vulva or vagina.

c. Roll the condom all the way down to the base of the penis before starting sex.

d. The boy should coat the condom with a spermicidal jelly or foam before sex. This will make the outside slippery and keep the condom from tearing. *Don't* use Vaseline or vegetable oil for this. These things make the rubber break down.

e. The girl should put the spermicide into her vagina before sex, using the applicator that comes with the tube or can. This combination of spermicide and a condom, used together, gives very good protection for *both partners* against STDs.

f. The boy should pull his penis out soon after

* Adapted from Robert Hatcher, *Contraceptive Technology 1986–1987.* 13th ed. (New York: Irvington Publishers, 1987); and Marsha F. Goldsmith, "Medical News and Perspectives," *Journal of the American Medical Association* 257, no. 17 (May 1, 1987).

climax, before it gets soft, holding onto the rim of the condom so it doesn't slip off. This will prevent any direct physical contact that might let STD germs pass from one person to the other.

g. Don't use the same condom more than once.

Using a condom and a spermicide is just another part of *living defensively*—protecting *yourself*—against contact with STDs until the time you and your partner are ready to establish a more permanent relationship. Of course, there are all sorts of reasons and excuses you can find for *not* using condoms, if you really work hard at it. You don't happen to have one handy, you say. It's a big, fat bother—who wants to stop and put one on just when things are getting interesting? The boy complains that sex just doesn't feel as good if you're wearing a condom. The girl complains that sex just doesn't seem *spontaneous* if you stop to put one on. A girl tells herself that if she carries a condom around, it makes her look like she's ready to go to bed with just about anybody anytime. If a guy has one in his pocket, it looks like he was just out for sex in the first place. And so on into the night. Well, let's be honest: these are just excuses. What *is* true is that to go the self-protective and common-sense route of *always* using a condom, *somebody*—either the guy or the girl—has to really insist on it, and it's likely to be the girl who has to do the insisting. As one girl put it, "If he says he doesn't have a condom, you just have to take a deep breath and tell him to go get one. No glove, no love."

GETTING MEDICAL HELP

Living defensively is by far your best protection against STDs. But if you haven't been living defensively, or if you think you may have caught a sexually transmitted disease anyway, it's important to protect yourself by getting medical help immediately.

DANGER SIGNS

- ABNORMAL DISCHARGES
- PAINFUL OR BURNING URINATION
- SORES, BUMPS OR BLISTERS ON GENITALS
- ITCHING IN GENITAL AREA
- ABNORMAL MONTHLY BLEEDING
- PAINFUL INTERCOURSE
- UNEXPLAINED SKIN RASHES

In earlier chapters we have talked about clues to look for. Any unusual discharge from the vagina, any painful discharge from the penis, any sores appearing on or around the sex organs, or any unusual abdominal pain should make you suspicious enough to look for help immediately. If you can share the problem with your parents or with a family doctor who knows you well, this is the best place to start. If you feel you can't do that, then see some other doctor, or go to a Public Health Service STD clinic. Insist that your visit be kept confidential—this is your right.

If the cost of seeing a private doctor is a problem, there are other choices that won't cost you anything. All large cities and most smaller ones have city or county health departments interested in preventing the spread of STDs. You can find their telephone numbers in your phone book. Many of these city or county offices have their own sexually transmitted disease clinics where you can obtain diagnosis and treatment without cost. (If they don't have their own, they can tell you exactly where to go to find help.) Public health officials know that STDs are a serious threat to *everybody*. They don't want *anybody* to go untreated because of inability to pay.

Doctors, public health nurses, and public health social workers are all part of a professional team to help people who have STDs to get help. Their work is confidential. But wherever you go for medical help, the same things will happen. First, you will be examined by a doctor for evidence of infection. Then necessary lab tests will be done to determine what STD, if any, is present. Once a diagnosis is made, the proper treatment—often an antibiotic—will be started. And plans will be made to check you later to be sure the infection is cured and hasn't recurred.

In addition to this, a nurse or social worker will ask you about the people with whom you've had sex. They aren't just snooping or trying to get you in trouble, they need to contact that person so that he or she, too, can be treated—or you can volunteer to contact that person. This is the only way to stop or control the spread of STDs. Your cooperation in this is terribly important. After all, if you got an STD from someone, that person is *infected,* and may well be endangering others by spreading the infection—or may be in danger, himself or herself, from serious complications.

Most young people dislike seeing doctors, even if it's free, and nobody likes to pay medical bills. With STDs it is far too dangerous to take chances. It doesn't help to wait for them to go away, because they *don't* go away. They just stay and do more damage until they are diagnosed and treated. They can cause permanent damage and make a mess of your life, if you let them. They don't *need* to if you go get medical help when you need it.

10
"IT CAN'T HAPPEN TO ME"

You might be surprised to know that books like this one, written specifically for young people in their teens and older, haven't been around for very long. Just fifteen years ago, most teens got most of their *formal* "sex education" from high school sexual awareness programs, some of which were very good, others very poor. The textbooks used in such courses were often either dull biology books that didn't actually say anything specific about sex education at all, or else were specially prepared pamphlets and booklets written and edited to be as coldly factual—and uninteresting—as possible. The main thrust of these materials seemed to be "Tell the kids the facts, if you have to, but don't get them too interested if you can help it." There was very little supplemental reading available to help young people get to the heart of real and serious problems that were facing them—problems such as unwanted pregnancies, birth control, or sexually transmitted diseases.

As a result, many young people didn't get much from these school programs. In some places these classes became the laughingstock of the school, a good subject matter for snickers and jokes but not much else. Some teens were lucky enough to get straight, honest sex information from their parents, but in many cases such lessons were so hedged in with do's and don'ts, rights and wrongs, goods and bads, morals and immorals, scare stories and preaching that it seemed that every lesson turned into a sermon, and the kids just tuned out. Where they *really* got their sex information was from their friends and peers, loaded with popular fairy tales and misinformation, or from dirty jokes, or from "what everybody knows." Then, presently, as these youngsters started to explore the exciting world of sex relations in person, they got the rest of their sex education from the School of Hard Knocks—from unpleasant and sometimes tragic personal experience. It wasn't any wonder that many teens in those days got trapped into bad trouble with unwanted pregnancies and sexually transmitted diseases. They didn't have reliable sources of information, or very much commonsense guidance, and they just didn't know any better.

A CHANGE FOR THE BETTER

Today all that is changed. There *are* books like this one for the young people who want to read them. It's possible now for young people to start off on the adventures and dangers of adolescent life armed with facts, and some commonsense guidance along with them. The fact that such books are published and made available on library shelves suggests that young people are reading them. So naturally it would seem reasonable to expect that in recent years the number of unwanted teen pregnancies should be declining, and that sexually transmitted infections should be appearing less and less frequently among teenagers. Right?

Wrong. Nothing of the sort is happening—and, in fact, just the opposite. Unwanted teen pregnancies are

A sex education conference for teenagers helps to provide them with necessary information on sexually transmitted diseases.

epidemic all over the country, in small towns as well as big inner cities. The steady rise in the incidence of most STDs is largely in teen populations, and AIDS is a disaster waiting to happen to sexually active heterosexual teens.

Many recent studies tell us that most young people have better command of the facts about protecting themselves against STDs than ever before. They have the *knowledge* necessary. But study after study also shows that they are simply not putting that knowledge into commonsense practice. They are not changing their lifestyles in any way to protect themselves. They are acting as if the dangers just aren't there, as if defensive-living practices don't apply to them—fine, maybe, for the rest of the world, but nothing is going to happen to *them.*

Well, now, just hold it a minute. Let's look at just one example from the real world. Researchers recently surveyed several thousand male and female first-year students in colleges and universities large and small throughout Canada. These young people were smart enough to be in college, and old enough (late teens and early twenties) to be reasonably mature and sensible in their defensive-living judgments. Eighty percent of the young men interviewed, and well over half the young women, admitted that they were sexually active.

Of those interviewed, quite a large proportion of both sexes had had sex relations with five or more partners in the course of the previous year, and many of them with ten or more different partners. All of them were reasonably up-to-date on the dangers of STDs. Yet only a tiny proportion of the girls, and practically none of the guys, reported that they always—or even often—used condoms when having sex. Most of them didn't use any birth control methods, either.* You could almost hear

---

*N. E. MacDonald, et al., "High-Risk STD/HIV Behavior Among College Students," *Journal of the American Medical Association* 263, no. 23 (June 20, 1990): 3155–59.

these bright young people telling themselves, "Well, yes, you probably *ought* to—but nothing can happen to *me*."

Everybody reading this book should think about this. The unhappy fact is that yes, indeed, it *can* happen to you, and you'd better believe it. You may *imagine* that you are invulnerable, but the fact is that you're not—nobody is. Why discover that fact the hard way?

THE STORY OF KATHY Z.

Not only can bad things happen to you if you don't remain alert and wary, they can happen when you least expect them to, and in ways that you might never even dream of.

Not long ago I met a young woman whom I'll call Kathy Z., obviously not her real name. Kathy grew up in a small rural town of about 25,000 people in Montana, not the sort of place where you would expect danger to be lurking around every corner. In the early 1980s she was entering her middle teens, and she was very much like lots and lots of other girls her age—really not much different at all.

From the beginning, Kathy had been a rebel. She didn't get along very well with her parents—they were constantly trying to cram their ideas down her throat about what was right and wrong, and how she should behave, instead of the way she wanted to behave, and she didn't respond too positively to that. She was a little overweight and felt very self-conscious about it. And while she wasn't really unattractive, she *felt* like she was, and she certainly wasn't the kind of raving beauty that some of her friends were. Like so many other girls of her age, she didn't feel very good about herself, and her parents weren't any great help.

Kathy the Rebel began smoking cigarettes at the age of twelve, and fought a long, running battle with her parents about that. Then she fell in with a bunch of kids at school who were doing a lot of drinking, too—beer parties in the woods once or twice a week, and some hard liquor as well. The crowd didn't do any other drugs except for marijuana, but they did quite a bit of marijuana. At age thirteen or fourteen, Kathy became sexually active and started having sex with just about any boy in sight—without taking any precautions, of course. In fact, she developed quite a reputation. True enough, she knew something about the risk of getting pregnant that way, and she knew something about sexually transmitted diseases, too. She just didn't care much. She didn't think anything bad could happen to *her*. . . .

Oddly enough, for three or four years, Kathy Z. was absolutely right. Nothing bad *did* happen to her. She didn't get pregnant, although she had plenty of opportunity to do so. She didn't catch gonorrhea or syphilis or any of the other STDs anybody had ever heard of. She didn't get killed in a drunken-driving auto accident either, although a couple of her good friends did. And by 1984, when she was seventeen, she began to get herself sorted out a little—probably because she really was a very bright girl. She stopped drinking so much, worked to get her grades up a little, and settled down to going steady with Tim, a nice guy in her class who seemed to think something of her. Then, in 1985, at the age of eighteen, she and Tim got married, over the fierce objections of her parents, who had largely given up on her long before anyway.

For about a year the marriage went fine. She and Tim both dropped out of high school a year before graduation and went to work. She used birth control in order not to get pregnant for a while. They had some good times together. But bit by bit, things began to go sour, especially with their sex relationship. They started having fights over nothing, and sometimes the sex just wasn't any good anymore.

At first they always managed to kiss and make up. Then one night they had a long, knock-down, drag-out

116

confrontation, and Tim told her the real truth: he had fallen in love with a young man in town and wanted to go live with him. It seemed that her husband had been bisexual all along, without her knowing it, and had had affairs with several young men since their marriage.

Kathy Z. was floored. The two were divorced in 1987, but somehow she and her ex-husband remained on reasonably friendly terms. They even had sex together now and then "for old times' sake." But Kathy had heard about AIDS—her ex-husband's homosexual friends knew all about it—and because she was worried, she finally decided to have an HIV test.

The test result was positive. At the age of twenty, she was infected. At that time she had had no sign of any symptoms. When I met her in 1990, she still had no symptoms, but her T4 lymphocyte count had begun steadily dropping a year before, sure evidence that her immune system was beginning to crumble under the attack of the virus. She had begun taking zidovudine (AZT) to try to slow the progress of the infection. A new test taken just before I met her had indicated that her T4 cell count was recovering to some degree on the medication—the zidovudine was working, for now.

What will happen now to Kathy Z.? Nobody knows, least of all Kathy. She's twenty-three years old now. Maybe the zidovudine will keep the infection under control for years, maybe not. Maybe she'll stay free of symptoms—and alive—long enough for one of the newer anti-AIDS drugs now under testing to prove effective and help her. Maybe she'll even live long enough for a real cure to be found. And maybe not.

One thing is sure: like Kathy Z., we are all living in dangerous times. This book provides a great deal of basic information about STDs—information that you can use in order to live defensively and keep your life free of these infections. What you decide to do with this information is 100 percent up to you.

117

GLOSSARY

AIDS (Acquired Immune Deficiency Syndrome)—a group of late-stage disease symptoms that appear as an end result of infection with the Human Immunodeficiency Virus. This virus attacks lymph cells and causes an immune system deficiency, that is, a breakdown in the body's protective immune system. AIDS is the end stage of HIV disease, and its disabling symptoms result in death in a high percentage of cases.

antibiotics—drugs that kill invading bacteria and help the body cure infections caused by bacteria. Examples: penicillin, tetracycline, streptomycin, isoniazide.

antibodies—special protein molecules formed by the immune protective system to immobilize foreign invaders such as foreign proteins or viruses.

antibody assays—special blood tests to determine the presence or absence of specific antibodies in a person's bloodstream.

cervix—the narrow lower end of the uterus, or womb, connected to the upper end of the vagina.

118

chancre—the small, painless sore or ulcer that usually appears on the male or female genitals as the first sign of syphilis.

chancroid infection—an STD that produces a large, painful sore on or near the sex organs.

chlamydia—a common STD that is especially dangerous to girls because it can infect their Fallopian tubes and prevent them from having babies later.

condom—a thin latex rubber tube, closed at one end, that can be rolled down over the boy's penis before sex to help prevent STDs.

ectopic pregnancy—a fertilized ovum which becomes implanted and begins growing in a Fallopian tube or some place other than inside the uterus where it normally implants and grows. A dangerous condition that can lead to sudden internal hemorrhage and require emergency surgery.

erection—enlargement and stiffening of the boy's penis when he becomes excited about sex.

fallopian tubes—the tubes that carry ripened egg cells from the girl's ovaries to her uterus.

genital herpes—an STD caused by a virus that produces outbreaks of painful sores on or around the sex organs.

genital warts—an STD caused by infection with human papilloma viruses, or HPVs. These viruses are often associated with early development of cancer of the cervix.

gonorrhea—one of the most common STDs, caused by bacteria that attack the male or female urine tube, and/or a girl's cervix and Fallopian tubes.

hepatitis B virus—a virus that causes hepatitis B, or so-called "serum hepatitis," a dangerous viral infection of the liver. Transmitted by blood contact (as by dirty drug injection needles) or through sex contact.

Herxheimer reaction—a harmless but alarming attack of chills and profuse sweating that sometimes occurs when penicillin is first given to treat primary or secondary syphilis.

Human Immunodeficiency Virus (HIV)—the name scientists gave to the virus that causes HIV disease and finally results in AIDS.

human papilloma viruses (HPVs)—a large family of different viruses that cause warts of all sorts, including genital warts. HPVs are now believed to play a role in the development of certain cancers, such as cancer of the cervix in women.

immune system—a complex system of white blood cells and protein substances that helps the body fight off bacterial and virus infections.

infertility—the inability to conceive or maintain a pregnancy. Infertility can arise from many causes, but one major cause is scarring and obstruction of the Fallopian tubes due to STDs such as gonorrhea or chlamydia infections.

labia—the folds of a girl's external sex organs, just outside the opening of the vagina.

lymphogranuloma venereum (LGV)—another STD that causes painful swellings around the sex organs. Caused by a germ similar to the one that causes chlamydia infections.

opportunistic infections—infections that the body's immune system normally fights down but which become serious when the immune system is damaged.

ovaries—the female sex glands which produce ripened egg cells, or *ova*, ready to be fertilized by the male sperm.

Pap test—a simple lab test, taken during a pelvic physical examination, to detect early signs of cancer in a woman's cervix.

pediculosis—the medical term for an infestation with lice. Pubic or "crab" lice are often passed from one person to another during close physical contact while having sex.

pelvic examination—a physical examination of a woman's external and internal sex organs.

pelvic inflammatory disease (PID)—an infection, usually sexually transmitted, that attacks a girl's Fallopian tubes or uterus. Most often due to gonorrhea or chlamydia infections.

pelvis—the lowest part of the abdomen where a woman's genital organs (uterus, Fallopian tubes, etc.) are located.

penicillin—the first of the antibiotic drugs, discovered by Alexander Fleming in 1928, and developed for use as an antibiotic in 1940.

protozoans—one-celled animal-like organisms which cause such human diseases as malaria, African sleeping sickness, amoebic dysentery, etc.

scabies—an infestation by a tiny itch mite that burrows under the skin and lays its eggs, causing a fiercely itchy skin rash. Often passed from person to person during close physical contact while having sex.

scrotum—the small sac behind the boy's penis that holds the male sex glands or testicles where sperm cells are made.

semen—the male sex fluid containing sperm cells, emitted when the boy ejaculates during his sexual climax. Semen is a body fluid that may contain AIDS viruses in an infected person.

serological test for syphilis (STS)—a kind of blood test to detect antibodies against syphilis in a person's bloodstream. The presence of such antibodies indicates that the person has, or recently has had, syphilis.

spermicide—a chemical, usually in a cream or jelly, that kills sperm cells on contact. It also destroys many STD germs.

syphilis—an ancient and deadly STD caused by a germ called a *spirochete*. In the first or primary stage of infection, the spirochete causes a small, painless open sore, or chancre, on or near the sex organs. In the secondary stage of infection, the germ spreads into the bloodstream, causing a rash all over the body. In the third or tertiary stage, the germ can attack and destroy many body organs, including cells in the nervous system, and may finally cause death. The germ may remain hidden, or *latent,* in the body for long periods during the course of the untreated disease.

testicles—the male sex glands, located in the scrotum.

trichomonas—an infection, caused by a protozoan microorganism, that produces troublesome itching and discharge from the vagina.

urethra—the urinary canal, which carries urine from the bladder to the outside.

uterus—the pear-shaped organ (sometimes called the womb) in the woman's lower abdomen in which a fertilized egg cell normally becomes implanted at the beginning of pregnancy.

vagina—the tube, leading from the girl's external sex organs to her cervix, where the boy inserts his penis during sex.

vulva—a girl's external sex organs, including the labia and the entrance to the vagina.

yeasts—a group of fungus-related one-celled organisms usually associated with fermentation of sugar into alcohol. Some yeasts, such as *Candida albicans,* can cause human infections such as *candidiasis,* or "thrush."

FURTHER READING

Chase, Allan. *The Truth About STD*. New York: Morrow, 1983.

Corsaro, Maria. *STD: A Commonsense Guide To STDs*. New York: Holt, Rinehart and Winston, 1982.

Johnson, Eric W. *V.D.* New York: J. B. Lippincott, 1973.

Mandel, Bea and Byron. *Play Safe—How to Avoid Getting STDs*. Foster City, CA: Center for Health Information, 1976.

Nourse, Alan E., M.D. *AIDS (Revised Edition)*. New York: Franklin Watts, 1989.

————. *Herpes*. New York: Franklin Watts, 1985.

Turner, Charles F., ed. *AIDS, Sexual Behavior and IV Drug Use*. Washington, DC: National Academy Press, 1989.

Warren, Terri. *The Updated Herpes Handbook*. Portland, OR: The Portland Press, 1988.

Wear, Jennifer and Holmes K. King, M.D. *How to Have Intercourse Without Getting Screwed.* Seattle: Madrona Publishers, Inc., 1976.

Zinner, Stephen W. *Sexually Transmitted Diseases.* New York: Summit Books, 1985.

INDEX

125

Labia, 24, 56
Leeuwenhoek, Anton van, 16, 17
Lymphocytes, 27, 80, 81, 83, 117
Lymphogranuloma venereum (LVG), 58, 64

Macrophages, 27, 80
Monogamy, 60, 105

Needles, drug, 13–14, 80, 85, 87, 88, 101–104
Nongonorrheal urethral infection (*see* Chlamydia)

Opportunistic infections, 83
Oral sex, 27, 32, 74
Ovaries, 24, 27

Papanicolaou, George, 94
Pap tests, 63, 70, 93
Pasteur, Louis, 17
Pediculosis, 94–96
Pelvic inflammatory disease (PID), 11, 36, 59, 93
Penicillin, 19, 37, 53–55, 70
Penis, 12, 22, 24, 34, 47, 58, 66, 91, 106, 107, 109
Pimples, 18, 66–67
Pneumococci, 18, 34
Pneumonia, 18–20, 83

Pregnancy, 36–37, 55, 59–61, 68, 69, 85, 112–114
Prostitution, 56, 99
Protozoans, 22
Psittacosis, 58
Pubic lice, 94–96

Rashes, 47–49, 51, 52
Reinfection, 38, 56, 60, 62, 93
RNA (ribonucleic acid), 20, 78, 79

Sarcoptes scabiei, 96–98
Scabies, 96–98
Scrotum, 24, 58, 91
Semen, 80, 84
Septicemia, 19
Serological test for syphilis (STS), 28, 48, 49, 52, 55, 92
Sex education, 111–114
Sexually transmitted diseases (STDs)
    chancroid infection, 18, 63, 64
    chlamydia, 22, 57–62
    defined, 9
    diagnosis of, 27–30
    genital herpes (*see* Genital herpes)
    genital warts, 91–94
    gonorrhea (*see* Gonorrhea)
    granuloma inguinale, 63–64